Bracali and the
Revolution in
Tuscan Cuisine

Also by Roberto Curti
and from McFarland

*Mavericks of Italian Cinema:
Eight Unorthodox Filmmakers, 1940s–2000s* (2018)

*Riccardo Freda: The Life and Works
of a Born Filmmaker* (2017)

Italian Gothic Horror Films, 1970–1979 (2017)

Tonino Valerii: The Films (2016)

Italian Gothic Horror Films, 1957–1969 (2015)

Italian Crime Filmography, 1968–1980 (2013)

Bracali and the Revolution in Tuscan Cuisine

ROBERTO CURTI

Forewords by FAUSTO ARRIGHI,
ALDO FIORDELLI *and* ENZO VIZZARI

McFarland & Company, Inc., Publishers
Jefferson, North Carolina

All photographs courtesy Francesco and Luca Bracali unless otherwise noted.

ISBN (print) 978-1-4766-6981-6
ISBN (ebook) 978-1-4766-3159-2

LIBRARY OF CONGRESS CATALOGUING DATA ARE AVAILABLE

BRITISH LIBRARY CATALOGUING DATA ARE AVAILABLE

Front cover images *clockwise from top left* Francesco and Luca Bracali, relaxing outside the restaurant, and one of Bracali's signature dishes, the Chianina Beef Tartare (courtesy of Francesco and Luca Bracali); Bracali's cooking show in Cortona, 2017 (courtesy Terretrusche Events; photograph by Valerio Paterni)

Printed in the United States of America

McFarland & Company, Inc., Publishers
Box 611, Jefferson, North Carolina 28640
www.mcfarlandpub.com

To my adored wife Cristina,
who taught me about
all the beautiful things in life
I never even dreamed of.
Thank you, my love.

And for Luciano and Manuela

Acknowledgments

First and foremost, my most sincere gratitude goes to Luca and Francesco Bracali, whose support and help was nothing short of enthusiastic throughout the writing of this book. They have opened up to me, and discussed their personal life and career at length with disarming sincerity. Not only they are two individuals I deeply admire for their dedication to work, their willpower and their sheer talent; they have become also two dear friends.

Very special thanks to Fausto Arrighi, Aldo Fiordelli and Enzo Vizzari, who have contributed to this book with their own recollections of their dining experiences at Bracali restaurant. It is a pleasure and an honor to include contributions on the part of such prestigious food critics.

I am deeply grateful to Vittorio Camorri, of Cortona's agency "Terretrusche" (www.terretrusche.com), whose help was very precious in the making. Mr. Camorri provided a good number of images for the book, taken from the food & wine event "Chianina & Syrah" which Terretrusche organized in Cortona in March 2017, which included Francesco Bracali's cooking show. The pictures from this event were taken by photographer Valerio Paterni.

Thanks also to David C. Tucker, who thoroughly proofread the manuscript, and to the following: Giorgio Dracopulos, Simone Fracassi, Andrea and Fabio Montomoli, Frank Nickel, Valeria Piccini (Caino Restaurant), Junichi Shiba, Gaetano and Giovanni Trovato (Arnolfo Restaurant). Last and not least, thanks to all the dear and beautiful people who attended a very special occasion, on October 9, 2011, the day the idea for this book took form. That was a day I'll never, ever forget.

Table of Contents

Foreword
by Fausto Arrighi

I first came to Massa Marittima many years ago—a fascinating location, with its amazing cathedral and the Abundance Springs, the ancient water source which rose to notoriety because of its unique fresco depicting the bizarre Tree of Fertility, which caused many diatribes with the local curia. The pleasure of these Maremma areas does not end with the monumental architecture and its works of art, though, but it goes far beyond, and its extraordinary territorial morphology emphasizes its unique landscape and views, with the walled villages on the barely outlined profiles of the hill.

I met the Bracali brothers at the time when their parents Manuela and Luciano led the restaurant: a rustic structure with a kitchen that was firmly rooted in territory. Nothing special, sure, but certainly in line with the average Italian restaurants in the 1980s. Then Francesco and Luca took over. I often told myself that their misadventures could fill a book … and now that book has been written!

The two brothers radically transformed the place, and its rusticity has given way to the ultimate elegance, with gilded rooms and lounges for a selected clientele, which turned the restaurant into a small temple of *haute cuisine*.

However, at first I was a little puzzled, having expected another type of ambience. But, much to my surprise, I realized how comfortable I was. That was the great merit of Luca, a master in his role, a host who welcomes every guest to perfection and always suggests the right wine for the occasion (and Bracali's wine cellar is definitely worth its name!).

Foreword by Fausto Arrighi

Francesco could only be a self-taught chef, an artist of the raw material, whose dishes are as beautiful as they are tasty. He is blessed with an extraordinary creative urge. It is certainly not easy to make a creative cuisine which is also the expression of the chef's personality in a territory like Tuscany's Maremma, which has well-rooted, secular traditions regarding food, especially red meat and game. You really must have lots of love and respect for the products, but also imagination and the will to experiment: a difficult blend, and one which pushes you to dare a lot, which is something Francesco is not afraid to do.

Bracali's kitchen offers a vision of the present projected toward the future, in a journey that still has many marvels in store. Full speed ahead, Francesco!

Fausto Arrighi is the former director of Italy's Michelin Guide, *2005–2012.*

Foreword
by Aldo Fiordelli

My first time at Bracali's table dates back to 2005, during my second year as inspector for the guide "I Ristoranti d'Italia" published by *L'Espresso*. I was 28 years old, unlikely to be exposed as a food critic, and yet I asked my sister to accompany me. I didn't want to attract attention, but perhaps my secret intention was to avoid being observed, so as not to betray my inner excitement. For a newcomer like myself, having to review one of Tuscany's most important restaurants was not something that happened so easily, and Bracali was already a legend. The recent luxurious renovation of the restaurant contributed to a solemnity that upset me. Then, however, the mixture of delicacy and irony which I later realized were the trait of Luca Bracali's character, along with the encouraging effect of wine, softened the emotional tension that the respect for the story of these two protagonists of Tuscan cuisine had inspired in me. This is how Luca Bracali is: at first he is demure and cautious, so as to better study his guest; then, when the latter has almost accustomed himself to an English-style presence, he turns witty, to bring him out and establish with him a relationship as a house guest, rather than a customer. Luca's choice of wines has a mastery whose true value will be understood only at the end of the dinner. He has the sly awareness of someone who already knows where he will take his guest, sip after sip; but the guest will discover this Machiavellian design only with the last glass, and will be surprised, fascinated and, indeed, conquered, Machiavelli-style.

I still remember vividly two dishes from that dinner, more than ten years ago, as it happens when you taste something truly exciting. The pigeon in three cookings: the entrails in a fried dumpling, crispy outside and creamy inside, with all the sincere scent of the offal; the seared breast, pinkish and escalloped with scallops, "bastard-style" as Luigi Veronelli used to say about dishes which mixed meat and fish; and the roast leg, super classic, accompanied by a purée of turnips and truffles. Like every great classic, an extraordinarily timeless dish, which predated the fad of exploring the flavors of roots, especially in winter.

Then, a dessert. A tart with figs and cooked grape must, which at first may sound banal. But it was accompanied by a lavender cream and a Cinta Senese pork ice cream, and the chef's suggestion was to taste all the ingredients together. As I usually do when I taste a dish, however, first I had a try at them separately. The tart was cloyingly sweet. The lavender cream tasted almost like soap. And the Cinta Senese ice cream made me literally jump, with its meat pie flavor to the limit of rancid. But then, in that mixture of disbelief and amazement, my palate started to tell me something.... Could it be that...? I took a spoonful of the whole thing, and I discovered Francesco Bracali's genius. In that seemingly cloying tart there were all the warmth, the maturity, the tenderness and the sweetness of the arid and windy summers in Maremma, with the final toasted flavor taking you right into the pine woods. The Cinta Senese pork ice cream recalled the wild character of this extraordinary area of Tuscany, populated by sincere people, often rude, but with one face and one word only. Finally, the lavender, a touch that conveyed both the peaks of elegance of which the chef is capable, and his underlying sensitivity which gave expression to the women of Maremma. In that touch of lavender there was the image of elderly rural women sitting on the doorstep in the villages, in midsummer, filling with lavender small tissue bags that would be put in the drawer and scent the linen kits. Isn't this Italy?

With that touch, Francesco Bracali showed all his extraordinary sensitivity of character and as a chef. A sensitivity which allows him still today to blend ingredients and cooking techniques in a surprising way—even incomprehensible and almost always unsettling indeed, when reading the menu. He inspires a mistrust which he then not only overcomes but shatters, conquering the guest through the ability of those dishes to express a "tonal cuisine," as Gualtiero Marchesi referred to it, in which each ingredient finds its proper place in the orchestra of the dish as a whole.

In Francesco Bracali's house, kitchen is a language, the ingredients are notes to tune together, and cooking techniques are the instruments. I grin when I hear about Ludwig van Beethoven's deafness, because the Ninth Symphony, the Fifth Symphony, the Moonlight Sonata are certainly not works that were written by ear, but are the figment of the imagination of a composer who mastered music as a language. So is Bracali's cuisine. A cuisine of the palate, a symphony in the plate which cannot come only from tests and tastings, but from a chef's ability to imagine through his own taste and olfactory memory a new pairing, a new balance, an uncharted taste. And this is where Bracali is a master.

Aldo Fiordelli is editor-in-chief for Tuscany for L'Espresso *restaurant guide.*

Foreword
by Enzo Vizzari

Francesco Bracali and Massa Marittima: the low profile of visibility which unites the beautiful town in the heart of Maremma to its most illustrious son today is curious, almost inexplicable. Among so many, and so celebrated Tuscan villages, Massa—the boundary wall, the Cathedral, the Municipal Palace, the Fortress with the Clock Tower, the network of narrow streets in the old town ... perhaps does not attract all the visitors it deserves. Francesco Bracali, or rather the Bracali brothers and their restaurant, highly esteemed in the circle of insiders and authentic gourmets, are less acclaimed and attended than many other eating places of a much poorer quality.

Yet Bracali is undoubtedly what can be called a "great restaurant," and certainly in the group of the twenty or less that can be labeled as the very best in Italy, where nowadays *haute cuisine* is experiencing highest moments like never before. The growth of Bracali's restaurant has been steady and uninterrupted over the years: an innate talent, self-taught but with eyes and ears wide open to the world of cooking, Francesco is a mature and complete chef, but not at all satisfied with the results he has achieved; Luca directs impeccably the "*maison*," elegant without ostentation, and cultivates with passion a vast wine cellar, deep and personal like few others. What does Bracali lack? The desire to show off, and seek shortcuts for the media spotlights. A flaw? A virtue.

Enzo Vizzari is director of L'Espresso *restaurant guide.*

6

Prologue

In March 1997, the prestigious monthly food & wine magazine *La Cucina Italiana* dedicated its column *"Saranno famosi"* (They Will Be Famous) to a young emerging Tuscan chef, located near the small Maremma village of Massa Marittima: Francesco Bracali. The writer, Toni Cuman, emphasized the "well-conceived territorial cuisine, attentive to the new trends in taste," which Bracali offered in his restaurant, and briefly traced its history, from its origins as a family-run *trattoria* situated in a locality called Ghirlanda, at the foot of the Maremma hamlet; he then described its interiors and summarily reported its most important dishes and its tasting menus—from the "Tuscan" one to the "Chef's tasting menu," priced respectively at the rather remarkable price of 70,000 *lire* and 100,000 *lire*.

"That was the very first important magazine article in my career," Francesco Bracali recalls now with a smile. "Nowadays, it would seem the easiest thing in the world, but back then it was an adventure. I had to take the train and go to Milan, at several hours' distance, and do a photo shoot for Italy's most distinguished food & wine magazine. For a kid like me, born and raised in Massa Marittima, it was truly an adventure—in fact, an *event.*"

In retrospect, what strikes most about the article is the opening picture: Francesco Bracali—then only 26 years old—poses with *La Cucina Italiana*'s then editor-in-chief Paola Ricas and Toni Cuman. The scene recalls a famous passage of Carlo Collodi's *Pinocchio*, when Pinocchio is standing between the gendarmes after he is arrested. Francesco looks

Prologue

much younger than he is, still almost a child, pale and visibly nervous. He is wearing the typical *toque blanche*, the chef's white hat, and looks down on the table, concentrated on the small *lasagna* he is composing on the plate. You can almost hear his heart pounding faster as he is putting his heart and soul in it, as if it were a matter of life and death.

Given the column's celebratory tone, Francesco's worries—which he openly confesses to the interviewer, with disarming naiveté—would seem baseless, the price to pay for an inexperienced young man who takes his first steps to celebrity. And yet, the article concealed an unpleasant back-story, which Bracali would reveal only many years later to this writer.

In the end, my big adventure turned out a disappointing, bitter experience. At the end of the interview, the reporter looked me in the eyes and told me that frankly, in his opinion, I should have to change direction as soon as possible. Meaning that my concept of cuisine, my dishes, my whole professional investment were wrong. Restaurants like mine, he said, especially those located out of the big cities, rather expensive, and centered on a type of cuisine as peculiar as mine, simply had no future. "Your restaurant will close down soon, my boy," he said bluntly. Like that. I was shocked. I went back to the hotel with tears in my eyes, utterly desperate. The thought of all the sacrifices my family and I had gone through, the fear of not being up to the task, the delusions that abruptly vanished in front of that verdict without appeal ... all that made me breathless. I felt completely lost. I met that journalist several times over the following years, at events or press conferences. I was no longer able to greet him. And he just looked away.

8

ONE

Deep in the Heart of Tuscany

Once Upon a Time in Ghirlanda

Beautiful things are not always born for a purpose. Sometimes, it's a matter of chance.

Our story takes place at the gates of Massa Marittima, in the province of Grosseto, in the heart of Tuscany. At the foot of the hill where the village is set, right at the corner of the last crossroads of the road that leads to the Medieval village, there is Ghirlanda. The name means Garland, but one would not even imagine that those handful of sparse houses even deserved a name of their own, let alone such a pretty and evocative one. But tradition has that every piece of inurbated land, even the smallest settlements, be Christened with their own appellative—and the Tuscan countryside is literally filled with such little hamlets, the remnant of a rustic civilization of small farmers and workers of the land.

Massa Marittima is located in a land of reclaimed swamps and mines: the hills all around, aptly named *Colline Metallifere* (Metalliferous Hills), are the largest range in the Tuscan Apennines, located in the Western portion of the region. The range runs through four provinces: the Southeast part of Livorno, the Southern part of Pisa, the Southwestern part of Siena, and the Northwestern part of Grosseto.

Massa Marittima flourished starting in the 11th century, after the gradual decline of Populonia, once an important Etruscan and Roman town. The Populonia naval fleet had been looted by pirates and destroyed by the fleet of Constantinople, and the bishop relocated to Massa Marittima. The decision was a key event for the local community, paving the way for its urban and economic expansion.

Unlike the surrounding cities, which were under the rule of Pisa, Siena and Florence, Massa Marittima maintained an independent status after a brief period under Pisa, and from 1255 to 1337 it was a "*libero comune*" (free municipality). A tourist who arrives in Massa Marittima today will find all the main buildings located in the main square: the cathedral, the Praetorian Palace, the town hall, the marketplace, the mint and the public fountain. These monuments were all built in the early 13th century, a period during which Massa Marittima was at the height of its economic power. The high and newest part of town, on the other hand, reflects a different historical period. In 1337 Massa lost its independence and became part of the Siena *contado* (the region surrounding the city).

The Senese administrators were people who lived, and thought, in quite a different way from the villagers, and their main aim was to keep Massa Marittima under their yoke. An example of such policy is the Sienese fortress, known as Cassero Senese and built in the 13th/14th centuries, a testimony to Siena's will to keep the population divided, in order to prevent subsequent attempts at insurrection. As a result, the village is basically divided into two parts. The cathedral, also known as the Duomo of Saint Cerbonius, hints at such dichotomy in its very architecture: the lower part is in Romanesque Pisan style, while the large arch is a later addition in the Sienese style.

The Senese domination marked the beginning of the decline for Massa Marittima. With the fall of the Republic, the industries were ruined, the mines languished, agriculture was abandoned and many noble families moved to Siena. After the plague of 1348, which decimated the remaining inhabitants, the population was reduced from 15,000 to 3,000 individuals. Siena donated Massa to the Visconti of Milan. Another plague, in the first half of the 15th century, further reduced the population to about 400. In the early 18th century Massa Marittima appeared almost like a ghost town, with crumbling and smelly houses and the villagers suffering from marsh fever. The princes of Lorraine attempted to repopulate Massa and its surroundings on several occasions: many families moved in the area, the marshes of the Pozzaione and Ghirlanda were drained, a hospital was built. The draining was completed in the late 18th century by order of Leopold I Habsburg-Lorraine, Grand Duke of Tuscany: with the air now clean and healthy, agriculture developed again, and the industries and mining sites could reopen.

The surroundings are known for its geothermal energy which manifests in sulfur geysers. Less than twenty miles from Massa Marittima, the village of Larderello is one of the world's most unusual places. It is sited in a volcanically active area, with plenty of hot springs and explosive outbursts of steam, which earned the valley in which it is located the eerie name of *Valle del Diavolo* (Devil's Valley). In the 19th century, it became one of the first places in the world to exploit geothermal energy as a support to the local industry. In 1827 the French scientist François de Larderel invented a way to extract boric acid from the volcanic mud: his work was supported by the then-Grand Duke of Tuscany, Leopold II, who awarded him the title of Count and funded a town named Larderello in honor of Larderel's work, which housed the workers in the boric acid production factory. In 1904, the zone was the site of a pioneering experiment in the production of energy from geothermal sources, and in 1911 the first geothermal power plant was built in the valley.

As their name suggests, Metalliferous Hills are principally known for their various mineral outcrops—pyrite, chalcopyrite, galena and tetrahedrite—which were already known during Etruscan times. Extraction continued for centuries and reached its peak in the second half of the 19th century and first half of the 20th century before it began to decline rapidly. Again, as it had happened in the past, the activity of mining was mostly carried on by outsiders.

Even though it is located at the foot of the hill that leads to Massa Marittima, Ghirlanda has little to do with it. On the other hand, it is strictly connected with the old mining business. In fact, the first thing one notices upon arriving in Ghirlanda, on the left, is the now-disused station, the terminus of the private railway line. In order to service the mineral mining, a railroad route was built in 1900, from the port of Follonica, on the Tyrrhenian sea, to Ghirlanda: the 16 miles' route was inaugurated in 1902, and serviced both passengers and freight trains. During the crisis following the Great Depression, and with the collapse of mineral prices, the traffic drastically diminished. In 1933 a transportation route by bus was inaugurated, and from then on the railway was destined only to freight trains. From Ghirlanda rode the mining convoys destined for the port of Follonica, and from there to West Germany. It is not the only sign of German activities in the area: a few miles from Ghirlanda, one evening in June

1944, in the village of Niccioleta, the Nazis killed 83 people, on the road that leads to Larderello. During their retreat the German army destroyed the bridge on the rivers Pecora and Pietraia, thus interrupting the railway line. After the end of the war, the Commission for the reactivation of transportation services connected to private industry did not judge it necessary to fix, and the Massa Marittima-Follonica line was suppressed in 1948.

When Luciano and Manuela Bracali decided to invest their savings and take over the tobacco bar at the corner of the crossroads that leads to Massa Marittima, right in front of their gas station, they did not imagine that their purchase would mark the future history of their whole family.

The place was a historical landmark for the villagers. Partly tavern, partly grocery, tobacco shop and haberdashery, it was one of those stores that were so common in small towns, and which offered a little bit of everything to the local customers, from a glass of wine to a packet of cigarettes, from sandwiches to stamps and postcards.

On the other hand, in Massa Marittima everybody knew the Bracali family. Even before owning the gas station, they had always been in the transportation business. In the early 1900s they used to be wheeled cart drivers: Luciano's father, Gino, was in charge of the transport of pyrite and chalcopyrite from the mines. He was a clever entrepreneur, and from the wheeled horse-drawn wagon he would soon move on to trucks and buses carrying workers in the area, after the decline of the railway line.

Gino then sold the company to his brothers, and among his investments there was the building in front of the gas station; there, in 1965, after obtaining the license to sell tobacco and cigarettes, he took over a bar. The spot was just right: the crossroads was an obligatory passage from the hills to the Tyrrhenian sea. Over the years, various managements would take over. Luciano Bracali and his wife's plan was to restructure the place and then give it back to others in management, as a long-time investment. Meanwhile, though, the shop had to stay open, otherwise they would lose their tobacco and cigarettes retail license.

And so, in November 1983, Trattoria Bracali was born. "*Trattoria*," mind you, initially in name only. In Italy, the term "*Trattoria*" indicates an Italian-style eating establishment, less formal than a restaurant: there are no printed menus, service is casual, wine is sold by the decanter, prices are low, and the food is modest and homemade, but plentiful, consisting of a small selection of local recipes. *Trattorie* serve the typical kind of dishes one would also find at home, and are aimed at a steady, unpretentious clientele. At the beginnings, however, Trattoria Bracali was basically a bar where Luciano and Manuela also served sandwiches, wine and assorted groceries. Then, sometime later and out of necessity, it turned into a proper eating establishment. A simple place, serving simple dishes to people with simple tastes. At lunch break, instead of carrying their lunchbox from home, the employees from the local telephone company offices stopped there for a bite, and so did the road maintenance workers, the paramedics and nurses from the hospital nearby, the salesmen and commercial travelers.

On the wooden tables with cheap nylon tablecloths, the kind that you just need to wipe with a damp sponge, were served *spaghetti al sugo* (Spaghetti with meat and tomato sauce), *lasagne, rosticciana* (grilled-cook pork ribs and sausages), pork steaks with fried potatoes, a *Cotoletta alla*

Bar Trattoria Bracali, circa 1983.

milanese which was actually a thin slice of beef with breadcrumb coating, a far cry from the original Milanese-style veal chop. At work in the kitchen were Manuela, her mother Iginia and a female helper. It was a housewives' kitchen, for men who at lunchtime put their dish under their nose and only ask for something warm and hearty to swallow with a glass of red wine before going back to work.

To the people in Ghirlanda, *haute cuisine* was a concept as unthinkable as a UFO landing. In 1983 Gualtiero Marchesi, Italy's most famous chef, was already a true superstar, but the guests sitting at the tables of Trattoria Bracali never even heard of him, nor could they care less about it. Moreover, not even the Bracali family were much interested in the restaurant business. Manuela did not particularly like to cook: to her, it was just a job like any other, as it had been supplying fuel. The same about Luciano Bracali: indeed, it is ironic that he ended up managing a *Trattoria*, since 18 years earlier he had decided that, instead of being a bartender, he'd rather manage the gas station on the other side of the road. Between 1965 and 1983 he had been dividing his time between his job in Ghirlanda and the shifts at the blast furnace at the Italsider steelworks in Piombino: in his absence, it was Manuela's turn to take care of the business, with the help of their eldest son Luca, born on January 21, 1968.

At only 16, Luca found himself behind the counter at the tobacco bar, lending a hand to his mother and cutting bread and slices of ham for the customers. Not a particularly rewarding job, of course, but Luca quickly realized that it was part of his contribution to the family to go to the Trattoria every day, after school, and never complained about it with his parents. All this meant a price to be paid. No joyful romps with friends, no room for teen games or spare time to read or watch TV: the need for work in those difficult years erased any other kind of entertainment, or leisure. And it made a kid become an adult ahead of his time, putting him before adult responsibilities.

Luca understood quickly what were the priorities to address, those that would allow him to make his way in life: perseverance and dedication must not be overshadowed, ever. It was a life of sacrifices, and without any certainty on the horizon. Luckily there was his brother Francesco, four years younger, born on the last day of 1971, to give him a hand. Francesco as well was destined to become part of the family business, and leave aside so many dreams that fill the vivid imagination of a boy.

For the Bracali brothers, adolescence came and went in a flash. In

Luca Bracali and his mother Manuela in the kitchen, 1987.

Ghirlanda people grow up quickly: no time for daydreams, the main concern is to try to get by.

Two Brothers

In Massa Marittima, the mining school—focusing on mining engineering and applied science—was the most natural choice for a teenager who wanted to have the certainty of a secure future. Luca was no exception, but in his heart he would have preferred the classical lyceum. A quiet boy, posed, thoughtful, he was a serious type, but able to open up in sincere, contagious laughter. One would not tell that his true passion were motors and speed. On the other hand, Francesco was a shy and stubborn character, and nurtured passions very different from those of his peers: he loved art, music, fashion, drawing, dance. His teenage idol was Michael Jackson, for the enthusiasm, energy and creativity.

Stephen Daldry's cult film *Billy Elliot* (2000), inspired by the true story of dancer Philip Mosley, tells the tale of an eleven-year-old kid who dreams of becoming a professional dancer. It is about vocation and sacrifices, incomprehension and tenacity. At first the story of Francesco Bracali seemed to retrace the steps of that little son of a miner in love with classical dance. Francesco too enrolled in a dance school, but in a retrograde provincial village like Massa Marittima one is not allowed to cultivate such strange passions. A kid who practices dance steps instead of playing football with friends? Never let it be: the giggles, the teasings, the villagers' glances are weapons that hurt, as are the labels cut with the scissors of ignorance.

But Francesco was not intimidated by village small talk. He was obstinate and determined. Even though his story would take quite a different path, the love for dance was already indicative of someone who quivers to express his own creativity and artistic temperament, one way or another. Whatever it takes.

What is more, even though he was just a boy, Francesco Bracali knew what it means to take responsibilities. It was he who took care of his maternal grandfather, Giorgio, who had been forced to leave his barber shop after a stroke; Giorgio was ashamed of his condition, and did not want to be seen by anyone. The only person he wanted next to him was Francesco, "Checco," the beloved grandson who took care of him every day.

Years later, Francesco would dedicate a pasta dish to Giorgio, the *"linguine tonno e capperi,"* (linguine, tuna and capers) in memory of those Sunday mornings when his grandfather took him for a walk around town and to the main square, to a grocery shop owned by a man called Durando, for a morning snack.

> You entered Durando's store, and it was like going back in time: the half-open big can of tuna in oil, a slice of *mortadella* so big that it seemed to belong to some gigantic, unknown animal species, the bright red slicer, the various forms of cheese, the jars of pickles behind the cold cuts counter. And, well, let's say that back then there was not such an attention to hygiene as we have now. I remember that we went in, one Sunday morning, and there was no one behind the counter. Durando came out from the back and asked: "My little boy, how would you like your sandwich?" in a very direct way, as we do in Maremma. And I: "Dorando, tuna and capers, please!" And he replied: "OK, I'm taking a piss and I'll be right back!" (laughs) As if it was the most natural thing in the world. Can you imagine something like that nowadays?

At thirteen, after completing secondary school, Francesco asked his father to enroll him at the Art Institute in Florence.

To tell my father "I want to go and study in Florence!" was something unthinkable. It was like saying, "The aliens have landed!" He looked at me straight in the eyes and told me I could forget that. Not because he wanted me to work at the Trattoria, but merely because to him, like many, many parents at that time, a fourteen-year-old kid who grew up in a small provincial village was not able to live in a big city like Florence or Milan. Back then, these were considered worlds apart.

Francesco then opted for the commercial school in Massa Marittima. He attended it begrudgingly, and with generally poor results. He soon ended up hating it. Even at home the relationship with his father was problematic, fraught with anger and barely repressed rebellion. At fourteen, one day Francesco took a backpack, put inside it the shirt he liked the most, a blanket and a Swiss army knife, and ran away from home. A decision made after yet another discussion with his father.

Since I had bad grades at school, and I knew I was going to fail my exams and be flunked, my father kept telling me he was going to send me to work in the woods, chopping lumber, with the Sardinians—back then, all the lumberjacks working in the area around Massa Marittima were Sardinian immigrants. And I was scared, literally frightened about the idea, as it meant the end of all my dreams. I was too weak, and it was this weakness that he kept targeting. Until I became convinced that the only way to avoid my fate, for me, was to go away.

The escape lasted only two days, but it left deep wounds that would heal only after a very long time.

Francesco Bracali's experience at commercial school ended after only two years. It was an abrupt early leave, the consequence of another foolhardy decision with no second thoughts allowed. The straw that broke the camel's back was a quarrel with the chemistry professor. Chemistry was the subject Francesco liked the most and the one in which he excelled. "I did an oral test which I thought deserved an A+, and he gave me a B+. I went back to my seat very angry. Everyone had realized that the test had gone very well, and a classmate even tried to protest and take my defenses, but the professor did not change his mind. To which I said, 'To me, school ends today.' And so it was."

Luciano and Manuela insisted that their son finish at least the school year. Francesco obliged but, stubborn as he was, he did it his own way: from then on, he would return all his tests and homework completely blank, as if he did not even exist. But since several professors used to eat regularly at the Trattoria, the news reached his father's ears. "Only two days before the assignment of marks, the technical design professor came to eat, together with the other teachers, and told my father that in three months I had not delivered one single drawing." Those drawings were all at Francesco's home: he had always done his homework, but never delivered them.

Luciano Bracali did not take it well. If his son did not want to go to school anymore, fine: then he must start earning his living by working at the Trattoria. Luciano was convinced that a summer's worth of hard work would be enough for Francesco to put his head in place and return to school the following September, with his tail between his legs. He was wrong.

That was the moment when I realized that working in a restaurant's kitchen could be the outlet for my creativity. On the one hand, my parents were not at all happy that I did not even have a graduation, on the other they saw how hard I devoted myself to work. And they realized that, even though I did not have the slightest technical basis, staying in the kitchen was the natural complement to something I had inside, and that was coming out naturally and spontaneously, day after day.

Looking back at it today makes him smile: if Francesco Bracali arrived where he is today, part of the merit, although involuntarily, can be given to his chemistry professor. If he ever took a trip to Bracali's restaurant, he would be surprised by his ex-student's skills: as taught by the eminent Hervé This in his groundbreaking books such as *Molecular Gastronomy: Exploring the Science of Flavor*, culinary art is a matter of chemistry.

"Damn the torpedoes!"

"I could not even cook a scrambled egg. I literally started from scratch. Can you believe it?"

Nowadays, for a cook the imperative is to boast about one's mentors, influences, homages. A three days' stage at René Redzepi's Noma, or at some top-notch Basque restaurant, seem enough to make automatically a great chef, even though the time there was spent peeling potatoes. And whereas there are many great chefs who openly acknowledge that their experience at Ferran Adrià's El Bulli changed their life and their professional attitude about cooking—such as Massimo Bottura, the chef patron of Modena's three-Michelin-stars Osteria Francescana, or Moreno Cedroni, of the two-stars Madonnina del Pescatore in Senigallia—there are far too many young aspiring chefs who are content to stick with "creative" rereadings of traditional recipes, and play with foams and agar-agar like kids with Play-Doh, but in the end are unable to properly *mantecare* (stir) a *risotto*.

Even for those who have never tasted a single dish by Francesco Bracali, it would be sufficient to listen to him talk about his job—how to conceive and prepare a recipe, the choice of this or that specific ingredient and their balancing, the procedure employed to create a particular taste, texture or aesthetic effect—to understand his extraordinary technical skills. A preparation born on the field, day by day, year after year, handling and learning the raw materials, the processing and cooking techniques, the physical, chemical and organoleptic properties of food.

Apprenticeship, inevitably, took place in the family.

> Before I started working in the Trattoria, it was my mother and my grandmothers who did all the cooking. For instance, I remember that my grandma used to make fresh pasta. And I started to learn the basics by observing their work in the kitchen, quite simply. Trying to grasp the basics. It was a matter of learning fast, because it was not like being at school. They worked, I watched. And I was like a sponge. I wanted to know, learn, understand, absorb whatever would happen, to the slightest detail—even though back then it was common thought that women had to stay in the kitchen, at home but also in popular *osterie* and *trattorie*. The host was in the hall, meeting the guests and serving wine and food at the tables, while women were in the back, at the stove. Think that my grandma did not even want me to stay there, with them: it was a taboo territory for a male.

Whenever practice was not enough, and Francesco felt the need of more detailed explanations, cooking tomes came handy. The teenage aspiring chef devoured those textbooks, like a student preparing the most important school test in his life. To him, school lessons had never aroused such excitement, such a feverish desire to learn. In particular, the volume that became Francesco Bracali's inseparable companion during his apprenticeship, and marked his first baby steps in the universe of cooking, was Auguste Escoffier's *La Guide Culinaire*, which he had recovered in a long out-of-print edition from a second-hand book store during a trip to Florence. The name Escoffier is nothing short of mythical in the world of fine dining: a renowned French restaurateur and chef, Georges Auguste Escoffier (1846–1935) started collecting, writing down and sometimes updating the traditional French cooking methods that had been passed on orally from generation to generation. By leaning on the work of Marie-Antoine Carême, who had first codified French *haute cuisine*, Escoffier simplified and modernized the techniques and recipes. In his home country, he was known as the *roi des cuisiniers et cuisinier des rois* (King of chefs and chef of kings).

> The book was out-of-print, back then. Finding that old edition was a stroke of luck. It became like the Bible to me. I learned many passages by heart, and recited them as if they were old poems, whose obscure meaning became clearer and clearer, day after day. On that book, I learned a whole lot of basic notions, down to the most traditional ones, which to me were absolute novelties. So, beginning from the pages of Escoffier's work, I gradually started my path—let's say I built my personal, cultural and professional baggage—as a self-taught.

Meanwhile, the elder of the two Bracali brothers was increasingly fascinated by the world of wine and restaurants. As Francesco recalled, "I remember that Luca left for the military draft, and upon his return, instead of wishing gifts such as a motorbike or a vacation, he wanted to go and buy silver placemats, which are used at the restaurant still today. We were absolutely determined: we wanted to do this kind of job, and nothing else." Luca had always been intrigued by wine.

> I always considered wine as something different from a mere beverage. When you taste a new bottle of wine, it tells you so many things. It tells you about the territory where the vines grew and the grapes matured, of the people who cultivated it, of the year when it was harvested.... So, tasting wine means having a glimpse of a slice of life, because wine *is* a living thing, and it constantly evolves. It grows and matures, it becomes strong and complex over time, it reaches its apex and then it undergoes a slow and inevitable decline. The wonderful thing about wine is that it is never the same, it is a constant surprise, and—when it is a good wine—it is a joy to discover.

Luca attended the courses of the Italian Sommelier Association in Siena, while studying economy and banking sciences; eventually he abandoned the university, but he got a diploma as a professional sommelier. However, the passage from theory to practice was not so easy. Luca was lucky enough to find along the way a few mentors to help him mature his vision of wine, and, like Francesco, he learned from his own mistakes. "When I first put together a wine list, I thought that it would be enough to have wines from the various grape varieties," Luca recalls with a smile. "In Grosseto I met a man, Doriano Della Lucilla, who was the representative of wines for a number of producers, including prestigious ones such as Antinori. There was a wine group he represented, Santa Margherita, which had wineries all over Italy." Luca looked at the list of the company's products, divided by the different grape varieties in the various areas of Italy, and ordered six to twelve bottles for each label. "And I thought I had assembled a good wine list!" A few days later, Maurizio Menichetti, the sommelier-cum-owner of the distinguished restaurant Da Caino, a staple in Tuscany, came to dinner, and Luca showed up with his brand new wine list and a big smile on his face. He was sure he would impress his older colleague. When Maurizio opened the list, he was shaken by uncontrollable bursts of laughter.

"Then," Luca recalls, "he literally annihilated my so-called 'wine list.'" Systematically, and with that Tuscan irony tinged in poison which never misses a target, Menichetti explained to Luca all the things that were wrong with it—that is, everything. "I had simply put together different wines, with no criteria at all. It was like someone putting together an art collection, and buying cheap reproductions of paintings from the nearby department store, based on the different colors. I never forgot that day, but it was a life lesson."

After that humiliation, Luca started going around looking for wine and tasting it with a more conscious approach. In 1988 he attended for the first time Italy's biggest international wine and spirits exhibition, and one of the most important in the world, the Vinitaly in Verona: he felt like Columbus setting foot on American soil. He also read a lot, especially the works by Luigi Veronelli, Italy's most important enologist, and a reference point for the food and wine world with his books, such as *Il vino giusto* (1968–1971). Veronelli had taught a whole generation of Italian wine enthusiasts how to taste and appreciate wine. This, at a time when the wineries were just starting to organize under a proper commercial tutelage: the DOC (*Denominazione di origine controllata*, "Denomination of Controlled Origin") quality assurance label for Italian wines, modeled on the French AOC (*Appellation d'origine contrôlée*) designations, had been introduced only in 1963.

Il vino giusto begins with Veronelli's definition of "wine, and especially a great wine":

It is the result of a series of coincidences, not just fortuitous but not mathematical either. To its birth concur: The choice of one or more grape varietals, and their biological equilibrium, conditioned, in one and in the other case, by a series of meteorological conjunctures; the terrain, for the presence or absence of determined rare substances, and for its behavior in rain and dryness; the climate, with its components, among which it has great importance the quantity of sun that the vine could hoard; finally, man, who conditions its success with each and every act, from the cultivation of the vineyard to the so-called vinification.... So, to make a great wine, with constant organoleptic characteristics, not only the aforementioned four elements are all necessary, but the conditions of all four must always be the same. A great wine is a harmonic creature, so perfect that to destroy its balance it is sufficient not to substitute, but just to modify one of these conditions.

Those were words that Luca would take to heart.

At that time, however, in most restaurants it was unlikely to find properly trained sommeliers who knew even the basic notions about wine. Wine expert Silvano Formigli did a pioneering work as the commercial director of the prestigious Castello di Ama, to spread the knowledge of Tuscan wines. A historical winery in the Chianti Classico region, Castello di Ama was founded in 1970 and gradually rose to prominence thanks also to Formigli's work; nowadays it produces a Chianti Classico which ranks among the world's most prestigious wines. However, Formigli liked to recall a significant anecdote that had occurred to him in the early 1980s, and which says a lot about the state of things back then.

> In a restaurant in Modena I asked for a bottle of Chianti, and the waiter replied: "White or red?" Caught by surprise, I protested: "But Chianti is only red, and DOC since 1967. Maybe you have white wines produced in the Chianti area, but they are not Chianti!" The waiter replied: "I'm sorry to contradict you, sir. I have done this job for twenty years and I can assure you there is also white Chianti." I didn't know how to react, the people in my party were laughing in their sleeve knowing how close I was tied to the Chianti area and how well I knew it. I'm in the game: "Ok then, bring me a bottle of white Chianti!" He came back with a bottle of white wine, from Villa Antinori. I said: "You see? This is white table wine, maybe of the Chianti area, but not a white Chianti!" And the waiter went mad: "So, what the hell did that seller tell me...?"

Formigli was an important character in Luca Bracali's maturation as a wine expert. In the late 1980s, Luca had assembled about 100 labels in the wine list; one evening he took advantage of a wine tasting event presided by Formigli in the village of Porto Santo Stefano, about one-hour-and-a-half drive from Massa Marittima, to show up and ask the expert to take a look at the wine list and tell him his opinion. "Think that I didn't even knew where this village was! But I had to meet the man, at all costs, and find out if I had done things well this time...."

He hadn't.

After the event, Formigli agreed to view the list ... and started criticizing it, in front of everybody.

> This time the substance—that is, wines—was OK. It was the form that was wrong, the way I had divided the labels and written them down. And he literally explained to me exactly how a wine list must be written, and which are the basic rules. I was

totally unaware of that. For instance, he taught me that the wine labels must be divided by areas. For instance, speaking of Tuscany, we have different areas: Bolgheri, Chianti Classico, Montalcino, and so on. Within each zone, you must put the name of the winery in alphabetical order; for each winery, the name of the wines; each wine, from the younger to the older. And this, not just for each Italian region, but for foreign countries as well.

Think of Australia, think of Napa Valley, which has sixteen sub-AVAs within it.... Or, take Bordeaux: it is too easy to simply gather the wines from that area under the term "Bordeaux," but when you drink a Bordeaux from Médoc and one from Saint-Estèphe, it is not quite the same thing. Even "Chianti Classico" has a variety of sub-areas, which mean different types of products. This means you have to do a thorough research in order to present the guest with a properly compiled wine list. Trouble is, nowadays as well only a few sommeliers use this method, and wine lists are often confusing to read, to say the least.

The two brothers' resolution infected their father. Luciano Bracali did not have the vocation of the restaurateur, but nevertheless he was a man who wanted to do his job as best as he could. When he embarked on a project, there would be no excuses: he must give his best and achieve the goal, whatever the cost. "My father was the only person who, once he understood that the restaurant was the thing that really mattered to us, trusted us at every moment," Luca explains. "And this even though there were also lots of arguments. But when it came to supporting us, protecting us, giving us confidence, he was ready. He was there for us."

So, when Luca told him it was necessary to prepare a wine list, Luciano accepted, even though the idea of keeping more than a handful of wines in stock would seem bizarre at the beginning. He probably did not have a clear idea of the amount of bottles that his firstborn intended to collect in order to compose his ideal wine cellar. But he realized this very soon, once the suppliers started arriving with their trucks, loaded with bottles. "It ended up with my dad being all day in the cellar, mounting shelves," Luca smiles,

because there was always the need to add more shelves to accommodate all the wine that kept coming! One day, early morning, we were both there, filling with bottles a line of shelves that he had mounted the day before, when a particularly imposing load arrived. My mother shouted from above: "Luciano, forty-eight more packages!" ... and I saw him raise his eyes to heaven, disconsolate ... he had to start again and mount some more shelves. Like the ordeal of Sisyphus, you know? Ceaselessly rolling a rock to the top of the mountain, whence it would fall back on its own weight ... and then start all over again!

The attempt to become a "real" restaurant was backed up by the economic strength of Trattoria Bracali. The profits were consistent, not the least because the patrons did not ask for selected ingredients in their plate or fine wines by the glass. To turn these secure profits into investments for the future was not something you do lightly. Because, as an old saying goes, when you leave the old road for the new one, you know what you leave behind but you don't know what you are going to find. Bracali knew that saying very well, but decided to place a bet on his sons. To him, a man who loved fast cars and the thrill of watching the scenery whizzing by steeply, leaving behind landscapes and thoughts, chasing the future when you are not yet satisfied with the present, it was like getting in a brand new car, with a powerful motor, and driving to an uncharted route.

It was a bet that everyone thought was lost at the start. Because everyone—banks, accountants, acquaintances, friends—were against them. But there was no going back. To paraphrase the words of Admiral Farragut, "Damn the torpedoes! Full speed ahead!"

The Sorcerer's Apprentice

The first fruit of the new road, the first dish born from Luca and Francesco's ideas, was a zucchini flan on a tomato cream. A very simple dish, even elementary, but a quantum leap compared with the traditional home cooking they were used to serving the guests, and one which filled them with pride. It was the first dish that they really felt as their own, the first stone in the new building that they were about to raise.

Switching from sandwiches and re-heated *lasagne* to "creative" dishes was not easy. This was Italy—or rather, this was Ghirlanda, near Massa Marittima, a tiny spot in the chart as far away as possible from the places where fine dining had become a not-so-uncommon concept.

The winds of the French Nouvelle vague in the restaurant world, the so-called *Nouvelle cuisine*, had started blowing late in Italy. This revolution made with pans and ovens was started by such eminent names as Fernand Point, Michel Guérard and Paul Bocuse, while the theoretical framework of this new trend that upset the heavy tradition which drew from Escoffier was made by Henri Gault and Christian Millau. By coining the successful formula "Nouvelle cuisine," the two journalists and food critics went to great lengths to publicize and spread the concept in the gastronomic world and in public opinion as well. Gault and Millau came up with a brilliant idea: a list of "ten commandments" which the followers of the new movement must obey.

The new tendency revolved around a simpler and lighter type of cuisine, which rejected the complex, caloric traditional dishes, reduced drastically the quantity of portions, and aimed at shorter cooking times, with the elimination of too long and overly elaborate preparations. This meant getting rid of fat and heavy ingredients, and replacing them with tasty and more digestible ones, for healthier and more balanced menus. To reach that goal, it was necessary to experiment, whether it be in cooking techniques, in the choice of raw materials, or in the pairing of ingredients. As for cooking, steam cooking and grilling would guarantee to keep the food's organoleptic qualities, whereas deep-fried cooking was almost totally banished. As for ingredients, for instance, pairing fruit with fish or meat, or using aromatic herbs instead of fat dressings, would guarantee a tasty but lighter result, while fresh, seasonal ingredients were preferable to preserved ones.

The search for simplicity also influenced the visual appearance of the dishes. The presentations became more essential, the various ingredients would be arranged on the plate according to a principle of simplicity and order, freed from excessive, artificial aesthetics. Chefs dedicated themselves to the artistic quality of the presentation, inaugurating a trend yet established today which consists of having lesser quantities of food in large format plates to give the dish a light and airy effect. Even art and design impacted heavily on the appearance of Nouvelle cuisine, so much so that color became the protagonist of the dishes, which had to satiate the eyes as well as the taste buds.

The ambassador of Nouvelle cuisine in Italy was Gualtiero Marchesi. After perfecting his technique abroad in some of France's best restaurants, including the brothers Troisgros' in Roanne, in 1977 the 47-year-old Marchesi opened his own restaurant in via Bonvesin de la Riva, in his hometown of Milan. It was nothing short of a shock. Within a couple of years, Marchesi's restaurant had been awarded two Michelin stars, and Gault and Millau put it among the world's fifteen best in a 1979 interview in the *Time* magazine. He became Italy's most famous chef.

In 1980 Marchesi published his book manifesto, *La mia nuova grande cucina italiana* (My New Great Italian Cuisine). People came from all over Italy and abroad to taste his signature dishes: *Riso, oro e zafferano* (Rice, gold and saffron), a *risotto* with an edible gold leaf on top of it, and *Raviolo aperto* (Open ravioli), a large, silky pasta sheet folded loosely around steamed scallops, and glossed with melted butter and a sprinkle of grated Parmesan cheese. The name Gualtiero Marchesi was popular even among those who never set foot in his restaurant—although the common conception was that, after dining at Marchesi's, one would be still so hungry than a pizza was needed to satiate the appetite. Sadly, it is a misconception that accompanies *haute cuisine* still today.

Other chefs followed, and gradually fine dining took place in big cities and in more provincial ones, thanks to a small army of bold innovators: Gianfranco Vissani in his family restaurant in Baschi, Umbria; Valentino Marcattili at the San Domenico in Imola; Igles Corelli, Bruno Barbieri, Italo Bassi and the Leoni brothers at the Trigabolo in Argenta, near Ferrara…. But in the deepest province, in a little village near Grosseto, poorly served by roads, the bet taken by the Bracali family was, to everyone, nothing short of a utopia. Indeed, to speak frankly, it was sheer madness.

The regular guests who attended the place formerly known as Trattoria Bracali did not understand the need for such a change. Even worse, they took it quite badly. "Who do they think they are, these Bracali guys?," "Did they get a big head?," "What are they hoping to achieve?," "Who would be so foolish to want to go along?," "Don't they realize this path leads to a foretold disaster?"

These and other questions were also uttered by friends of the family, and seemed to have no immediate answers. But Luciano was aware of his sons' talent and skills, and he stubbornly chose to stand by them in public—even if in private, when no one would hear him, he would criticize each stumble, each little daily failure. As a consequence, Francesco and Luca's relationship with their father remained difficult. They both felt he was an invaluable support, but at the same time he was a stern judge, the most severe of all. There was no room for missteps, which would inevitably occur with time, in what was essentially a route of trial and error. Without those missteps, life would have been much easier, but probably the two brothers would not be where they are today. Most importantly, they would not have become the persons they are.

Francesco Bracali's growth as a chef went through several stages, marked by the meeting with leading figures in the history of Italian cuisine. The first was Angelo Paracucchi, the owner and chef at the Locanda dell'Angelo in Ameglia, where Francesco spent his first and only professional stage in a kitchen staff, in 1990. "To this day, I consider Paracucchi one of the true great chefs of Italian cuisine," Bracali recalls.

He was a cook in the most classic sense of the term. Whereas Gualtiero Marchesi was an experimenter—the open ravioli or the gold leaf saffron *risotto* were nothing short of revolutionary, at a time where all of us cooked, and ate, *lasagne* and spaghetti. Sure, nowadays they look like simple, basic dishes, but back then, Marchesi was like a Martian to us. Paracucchi, on the other hand, represented classicity, and elegance.

Born in Cannara, near Perugia, in 1929, Angelo Paracucchi had studied agriculture at high school and then left Italy to discover European cuisine; after he returned to his home country he started working as a hotel manager and a maître, before his true passion—cooking—took over. His rise to fame came as the chef at the Agip Motel chain owned by the Italian oil and gas company ENI, particularly the one in Sarzana which in the late 1960s and early 1970s became one of Italy's few reference points for gourmets all over the nation, despite being located in an area (between Tuscany and Emilia, near the Tyrrhenian sea) away from the main routes and motorways.

Paracucchi was indeed a forerunner, and not merely that. He was one of the first chefs who crossed the threshold between the salty and sweet, by putting fruit into fish and meat dishes; he experimented on the change of textures, and his "lettuce sauce" can be considered the ancestor of today's liquid salads; he investigated the biochemical structure of food, not only to preserve their organoleptic characteristics, but also in order to make them healthier (he was often the main guest at conferences on nutrition, and named a dish "health salad"); and he was one of the first who fought for the integrity and the valorization of local products such as the extra virgin olive oil. On the other hand, Angelo Paracucchi was perhaps the first example of restaurateur-cum-entrepreneur, who broadened his horizons abroad, being the first Italian chef to open a fine dining restaurant in Paris, the "Carpaccio," and in Japan, the "Angelo Paracucchi" in Osaka; he became also a TV celebrity, appearing in the broadcast *La Meridiana* (1980). He even launched and commercialized his own products, such as a popular line of sauces; last but not least, he was also a designer, and created a special cooking pan.

In 1975 Paracucchi opened his own restaurant. Within a few years, the "Locanda dell'Angelo" ("Angel's Inn"—the name being a wordplay between the word "angel" and Paracucchi's own name) became one of the strongholds of what would be known as "New Italian Cuisine" between the 1970s and 1990s: a research lab, a forge of new dishes and a starting point for young talents. The choice of a small village in the Tuscan area called Lunigiana seemed a debatable choice at first, but Paracucchi was adamant about the reasons behind it:

> Even though Milan has probably the best food market one could hope for, both for the freshness and the variety of products, to someone like me these privileges are not enough. I can find the same things here, at the Locanda, right on my doorstep. For instance, I can buy sea bass from the local villagers who go fishing as a hobby. As for vegetables and mushrooms, I pick them up from the stalls of the nice old ladies who sell them at the market to supplement their pension. And on the street I meet friendly people who stop me for a chat about my latest TV broadcast or a newspaper article about me they just read. On top of that, the sequence of the seasons, for both the kitchen and the landscape, still makes sense here.

To Francesco—a self-taught, 19-year-old aspiring chef who had never been in a professional kitchen before—, the stage at the Locanda dell'Angelo was nothing short of a shock.

> The main problem was my inexperience. Quite simply, I did not have the basics, I was not prepared to fully absorb what Paracucchi was offering. And perhaps, because of this, I think I learned less than I could have had, at least in the immediate. Much of what I learned, I did over the years, on the field, trying, failing, trying again … anyway, it was a healthy shock, as it opened my eyes. I could finally see what a real *haute cuisine* restaurant was like, how a great chef worked inside that structure, organizing the daily routine and the kitchen staff. In short, what it was like to do this job professionally.

Perhaps the most important legacy of that period was learning the importance of raw materials. Those who accompanied Paracucchi early in the morning to the Pallodola vegetable market in Sarzana could witness some amusing skits, such as when the chef insisted that an elderly lady sell him the beans which she had already in her basket, because they were better than those he had found on the stall. The lady eventually obliged, as Paracucchi would not take no for an answer. He even had his collaborators set up "roadblocks" at 4:30 in the morning, in the country roads where he knew truck suppliers would pass, so as to be the first to choose the most delicious artichokes before they ended up on the fruit and vegetable stalls.

Bracali recalls vividly the daily visits at the fruit market, at 5 a.m.

> Paracucchi took us all there, and he would 'explain' the raw materials to us. Their basic characters, their nutritional role, the way they had to look, smell, taste, in

July 1992: Francesco Bracali (*center*) receives a diploma after his stage with chef Angelo Paracucchi (*left*).

their best possible form; how to choose them; how to detect a good vegetable from a less tasty one, and so on. It was like learning the alphabet anew. He was a phenomenal connoisseur of ingredients, perhaps the greatest I have ever met.

Then, for the young apprentices, it was the time to learning their craft on the field.

Paracucchi's sous-chef would prepare a menu, and at lunch we ate what we had seen him cook; then, in the afternoon it was our turn to test ourselves in the restaurant kitchen, trying to recreate what we had tasted. For each course, Paracucchi illustrated the ingredients and the preparation. He had a passionate approach, that went beyond the technique or the organoleptic quality of the aliments. It was not simply a matter of explaining the composition of foods, or their chemical changes depending on the different cooking and so on.... He was like a painter playing with colors, or a musician with notes. There was an emotional transport that came from within, which caught you, involved you, fascinated you.

Far more influential, in hindsight, was the advice of two already established colleagues, who for the young chef would become something more than just teachers: Gaetano Trovato, the chef owner of the restaurant Arnolfo, in Colle Val D'Elsa, and Valeria Piccini, the chef owner of

Bracali and the Revolution in Tuscan Cuisine

Da Caino, in Montemerano, Maremma—nowadays both are two-Michelin-stars restaurants as well.

Arnolfo is nothing short of an institution in Tuscany. It is also another restaurant founded and owned by two brothers, who, like Luca and Francesco, take care respectively of the wines and the kitchen. Giovanni and Gaetano Trovato, grown in Tuscany but of Sicilian origin, opened it in 1982, in one of the most beautiful medieval hamlets in Tuscany, in the Elsa valley. Gaetano Trovato had grown up in his mother's kitchen, and after a stage in St. Moritz he had started a path very similar to Francesco's; it was inevitable that he took a liking to that stubborn young man.

> I remember that on Tuesdays, when the restaurant was closed for weekly rest, I took the car and drove to Colle Val D'Elsa, which is about one hour and a half from Massa Marittima. Gaetano was the first to teach me how to make the dough for fresh pasta, and the result was very different from the one my grandmother used to do. I was starting to realize that home cooking is one thing, and restaurant cooking is another. The rules you have to follow are very different.

The Trovato brothers' restaurant took its name from Arnolfo di Cambio, a prestigious architect and sculptor of the 13th century, who was born in Colle Val d'Elsa and presented the first projects for the Cathedral and Palazzo Vecchio in Florence. The name also signaled the Sicilian chef's taste for architecture and art, which resulted in the way he composed visually appealing and extremely elegant dishes: "I like to call my kitchen an architecture which is continuously consumed and which has to be renewed every day," Trovato says. From him, Francesco understood also the importance of aesthetic taste, and the attention to the appearance and presentation of a dish, conceived as an architectural design which pleases the eye before the palate.

Valeria Piccini too followed a similar path as Francesco Bracali. She and her husband Maurizio Menichetti took over a family store opened by Maurizio's parents since 1971 in the minuscule hamlet of Montemerano, near the Saturnia thermal baths. At first Da Caino (the name refers to the nickname of Maurizio's father, Carisio) was simply a winery where cold cuts and cheese were served. It was only over the years that it gradually became one of Central Italy's most prestigious restaurants. By looking at Valeria, one would not think of her as a first-class chef: a big, matronly woman with a sweet smile, she looks more a loving mother who cooks dinner for her children. Francesco came across her during a visit at the

Vinitaly exhibition with Manuela, and recognized her immediately (who wouldn't?); like a kid who glimpses his favorite actress among the crowd, he could not hide his excitement. "Mom, mom, look who's there...! It's Valeria, the chef from Da Caino...." "Who? Where?" And he, in reply: "Right there, mom, the big fat lady! She's a famous chef!" Too bad Valeria was within earshot, and heard the whole exchange. She turned back and smiled: "Yes I am, the big fat lady, indeed!" Francesco sank into the earth from shame, but Valeria did not take it as an offense. It was the beginning of a beautiful friendship.

"Valeria used to call me in the days the restaurant was closed, telling me she had purchased some new stuff and urging me to come over," Bracali recalls. When he started taking lesson from Valeria, Da Caino had only one Michelin star (it would earn its second in 1999).

> Back then, Valeria used to purchase kitchen accessories from a company I did not know, located near Brescia, in Lombardy, which sold products for pastry: Artebianca. Today it is a famous name, and even Albert Adrià taught courses in its premises. There, she purchased all type of stuff: stamps for cakes, for instance. There were all kinds of them, even really kitsch ones, such as structures shaped like the most famous monuments in Rome, which nowadays no one would even dream of using, but which back then suggested an idea of opulence—and this might give you an idea of how the aesthetics in *haute cuisine* have changed over the years. There were also ice sculptures, silpat pads—those silicone pads that replaced baking paper—and so on...

Then, Valeria and Francesco proceeded by trial and error, as many of those items—nowadays widespread in every kitchen, but still elitist at the time—were still unfamiliar to them.

> Valeria purchased these accessories, and then called me to try them out together, and from there was born a friendly relationship that went beyond work. We kind of grew up together, professionally, even though I was starting from scratch whereas she was already a chef with a solid background. But it was really exciting to deal with this type of process together, using our spare time to experiment things, and discovering something new each time, even drawing inspiration from our own mistakes. We felt like explorers, and in a sense we were.

As with Francesco, Luca's training did not take place through the typical channels: it was a search on the field, which allowed him to develop his own ideas, culture and tastes on wine without accumulating prejudices or being influenced by other people's tastes and opinions. On the whole, he matured an extraordinary ability to "think" the wine, analyze it, understand it: a quality that would help him in the future, accompanying his growth as a sommelier, and forging his capacity to explain a wine, its story, its characteristics.

Last but not least, Luca found another mentor whom to call prestigious would be an understatement: Claus Josef Riedel, the owner of the company of the same name. Riedel (1925–2004) was the man who first understood that the way a glass is shaped affects the perception of the drink itself. He founded his firm in Austria, first working with glassmaker Daniel Swarovski. He studied chemistry, and spent 16 years studying the physics of wine, the way it is delivered to the taste buds, the story and properties of the various wine varietals. Since the taste of wine changes according to the shape of the glass that contains it, Riedel created grape-varietal specific glassware, designed to enhance the types of wine based on the specific properties of individual grape varietals. His first creation, the Burgundy Glass Cru, was exhibited at the Brussels Expo '58, and later acquired by the Museum of Modern Art in New York. Riedel's work on the design of wine glasses influenced the world of cuisine and wine tasting in countless ways: in 1973, his Sommeliers Series marked the birth of the world's first gourmet glasses.

Riedel knew Italy, and Tuscany, very well: he had been there during the war, in the German army, fighting the partisans. He had been captured in 1945 and sent to a POW camp in Pisa. He owned a villa in Follonica, just a few miles away from Massa Marittima, and spoke the language very well. He was an affectionate guest of the Bracali restaurant since its very first steps. He took a liking to Luca, and after dinner the two men often launched into long conversations about the different wine varietals and the various types of glasses, and how the same wine served in different glasses acquires different characteristics.

Such a relationship of friendship and understanding enriched dramatically the young sommelier's background. "Claus Riedel often came to lunch, alone," Luca Bracali recalls.

Great character. He was in his late sixties, but still a sporty type. He came to the restaurant (which back then was still a *trattoria*) atop his Harley Davidson motorbike, dressed in black leather from head to toe, and with a change of clothes in his briefcase. He retreated in the bathroom and reappeared with a suit and tie, impeccable. At the table, he always chose the zucchini flan with tomato sauce, and perhaps this is the reason why we still remember that dish with affection. And whenever he had a new collection of wine glasses to show, he called me and anticipated he would come straight from Kufstein, with his Volkswagen Golf 3000 full of wine glass boxes. Not that he was a great lover of wines, but he was a deep connoisseur of the matter, like no other I have ever known. Thanks to him I learned the characteristics of each type of glass, the best combination with the various wines, and so on.

It was thanks to experiences like this that Luca Bracali gradually acquired self-confidence, matured his own ideas about wine, and developed a well-defined personality in the field. He was not the classic type of sommelier: he did not fit at all in that set of clichés that are often associated with the profession.

When talking about a wine, he does not embark in flights of fancy on, say, dry leather bouquet, nor will he keep swirling the glass in one of the typically spectacular gestures which in his view are mostly exhibitionist. He does like to recall a moment he succumbed to wine swirling, in spite of his training:

> One night I had a dinner date with a girl. First date, and I was very, very nervous. We started talking about this and that, and I was lost in thought. Almost unconsciously, I started swirling the red wine in my glass. Faster and faster. Then, disaster struck. The nightmare of every wine lover: for a moment, I lost control of the glass, and poured the content all over the table ... and us as well—my shirt, her dress, everywhere. I think I became purple with shame, whereas she took it well, and laughed out loud. Then, to resume the conversation, she said: "But tell me more about you, Luca. What do you do for a living...?"

Changing Face, Shedding Skin

Shedding skin is a periodic renewal of all living beings. For some, it takes place in a more evident manner than others. Some reptiles just climb out of their old skin, leaving it behind in one place. We humans shed our skin continuously—1.5 million skin cells every hour, with a new skin surface every 28 days or so—although we don't realize it. But we shed it also figuratively, during our personal maturation, whether it be in our relationships with others as well as in the daily confrontation with our own selves.

Shedding skin is an essential moment in order to grow. A gradual, sometimes painful process. And since a restaurant can be compared to a living organism, and a rather complex one too—the product and the summation of those individuals who have created and sustained it with their creativity, dedication, money and work—it too has to undergo such a path. When Francesco and Luca Bracali decided to take the big leap from their parents' *trattoria* to a fine dining restaurant—something unheard of in their area—they understood that this would be a necessary step, if a drastic and painful one.

Replace the tableware. Expand the wine list. Choose glasses suitable to the types of wine served. And, especially, renew the menu—drastically and even dramatically. To ban the pasta, the grilled meat, the *ribollita* soup, was nothing short of a revolution, and one destined to turn away the majority of the local clientele. In the early 1990s, in such as small Tuscan village, the average Joe who sat at the gingham tablecloth of Bracali's place just wanted a big dish of *spaghetti al pomodoro* to fill his stomach and a glass of red wine—no matter the label—to accompany it, and could not care less about anything else remotely resembling a deviation from the safe path of traditional dishes and tastes.

Francesco Bracali knew he and his brother were making a somersault without a net, but he also knew it was the only way to evolve, and to come up with an approximation of his idea of a restaurant. So, he went against the tradition, and rebelled against techniques and recipes that were being handed down from generation to generation, like the long cooking, and the use of heavy sauces and dressings. The cooking had to be brief, in order to preserve the flavor and texture; the dressings would be light, so as to keep the dish easily digestible and not overly caloric; and, last but not least, each dish would be prepared and presented with an eye to an element previously unthought of: aesthetics.

What is more, shedding skin also had to be a radical change of attitude on the part of the restaurateur. "Making my father understand that we would have to open at 12:30 for lunch and at 8:00 p.m. sharp for dinner, absolutely, was a disaster. To him, if someone showed up at, say, 11:30 in the morning or at 6 p.m., for a sandwich, you had to feed them. He did not understand that, if we wanted to become a 'real' restaurant, we had to have precise opening hours." Another step was the staff having dinner all together, before the start of the evening service, instead of eating separately and in the spare time between one guest and the other. "We had to learn and practice discipline, and start from scratch."

The skin change extended to the clientele as well. It was a necessary selection, although one subject to misunderstandings and collateral damage. Bracali's average guests were either truck drivers who stopped by during a trip, or the guys at the local telephone company. Having to say no to the clerk who turned up at twelve o'clock for a ham sandwich because his lunch break only allowed him to stop by at that hour, meant losing a customer, because he would not be back one hour later: he would just have lunch at another place.

But there was more. Once your guest is sitting at your table, set with elegance and taste; once you have served him a quality wine in the perfect glass to taste its nuances, and a dish conceived and prepared to enhance the product and preserve the taste and harmony of the ingredients, with the added element of creative reworking that makes that dish something unique and, most of all, *yours*, because its conception reflects your idea of cuisine; once you have achieved all that, behold, because it is not at all certain that the guests will appreciate all this. Not at all certain.

An exemplary test was the pigeon. In rustic Tuscany, pigeon is one of the most popular main courses. The baby pigeon (or squab), never any older than one month old, is roasted or cooked on a spit, its crispy skin concealing the sweetness of the red, tender meat. It is seasoned, and sometimes its breast cavity is stuffed with a mixture of herbs in order to highlight the flavor. The whole bird is traditionally served on the plate, and must be eaten with one's bare hands—fork and knife would be useless to debone it.

"Never, ever my parents would think of deboning a squab beforehand and cook the single parts separately," Francesco explains:

> to them, pigeon was either roasted or stuffed, and there had to be the whole of it, bones and everything. And it was not just them. In Tuscany, in every single restaurant, the pigeon was cooked the traditional way. It was like the Gospel, you just could not change it. Why, I asked. Because it has to be *like that*, they replied. It was a vicious circle.

Francesco wanted to try something different.

> Basically, it is a matter of knowing the animal and its characteristic. The different parts—the breast, the thigh—need different times of cooking, in order to preserve the taste and the texture. When you get the whole pigeon at your local tavern, you have a potentially wonderful dish which is usually ruined by the extra time in the oven or on the spit. You have the shadow of what it could have been, like the shadows in Plato's cave.

So, Francesco started to study the pigeon. Debone it, cook the parts separately, keep the breast pinkish, leave the meat to rest so that the juices would concentrate on the inside and expand once the temperature goes down. And serve it in a way that would be pleasant to the eye as well. It was a small revolution in itself.

Bracali and the Revolution in Tuscan Cuisine

When Francesco presented "his" pigeon to his most trusted guest, Claus Riedel, the king of crystal appreciated, and how. But many others, accustomed as from the rural tradition to have the whole carcass on a plate, its meat almost burned and the skin greasy with oil and fat, and to rip the flesh off the bones with their teeth, turned up their nose. What was *that*? And *why*?

What to do, then, when someone who pays money to taste your food does not have the slightest idea of the effort that is behind all that? What to do when the guest thinks that by paying a higher sum he is entitled to, say, a whole bowl of spaghetti instead of three small ravioli, or to a whole pigeon instead of the sole breast and thigh resting in the center of the plate, looking a bit lost—not to mention the meat looking suspiciously red instead of well-cooked?

To a chef, cooking is also communication—expressing his (or her) ideas and vision of the world. To Francesco, it meant showing that there could be a different way to approach traditional cuisine, and improving upon it. But, how long would it take before he would finally find an audience willing to share his vision, and trust him?

New Year's Eve, 1992. When the first dish returned to the kitchen, untouched, Francesco became a bit nervous. Perhaps he had expected, or feared it. When the next one turned up, untouched as well, he felt the metallic taste of fear in his mouth. At the third untouched dish, he was in a cold sweat. He had prepared the menu carefully, he had studied every single detail, he had tried hard to make a good impression, and make that evening an unforgettable experience for his guests. It was a special occasion. People who never move out of their kitchen for the whole year choose New Year's Eve to go out to dinner and celebrate an end and a new beginning. They want to treat themselves royally. New Year's Eve dinner means abundance, opulence, wealth in the pot. And what could be more opulent than *foie gras*, the "rich" food par excellence, caloric and jelly-like, a pre-libacy that dates back from the times of Pliny the Elder?

For the first time since he started cooking professionally, Francesco had created a foie gras dish. He had marinated the goose liver with Sauternes, and paired it with dried fruit. Nowadays, it sounds like the most classical, simplest, harmonic and fulfilling proposal a fine dining restaurant can offer on the theme; the more snobbish gourmets, always looking for some surprising palatal shock, might even be bored by it, as if they were rewatching an old black-and-white movie for the umpteenth time. Whereas the guests sitting at the tables of the Bracali restaurant during the New Year's Eve dinner did not yawn, not at all. But they were left with their mouths open, and not out of joy.

That evening, no one ate that foie gras *au Sauternes*. And a similar fate awaited the chicken galantine, as well as any other of the dishes conceived by Francesco for the evening's tasting menu. The plates were ruefully returned to the kitchen, barely touched by the odd adventurous customer. Francesco was crying with anger. And when his father Luciano showed up at the tables to ask if everything was OK, one guest curtly replied: "If the rest of the dinner is going like this, we're having a pizza somewhere else afterwards."

That foie gras defeat deeply marked Francesco Bracali's style. Stubborn as he is, he made that ingredient an essential component of some of his most complex dishes, such as the Livornese chicken salad with foie gras pudding, cooked grape must and parmesan cheese ice-cream, or the nettle gnocchi, where the foie is once again transformed into a pudding lying on the bottom and surmounted by a rain of chopped hazelnuts and caramelized onion. The foie returns, significantly, in another signature dish: the pigeon. A touch of foie, so sweet and soft it melts in the mouth, accompanies a quenelle of the bird's raw fillet. The bite of the gods, a surge of additional, unspeakable pleasure to top an already masterful creation. And, perhaps, a way to leave a sweet taste in the chef's mouth as well, and clean away the bitterness of a long-lasting memory.

Two

On the Way
to the Stars

A Young Restaurateur's First Steps

Little by little, Bracali restaurant started to gear up, with great difficulty and amid general mistrust. The fact is that the young chef from Massa Marittima—self-taught, without any specific technical background, with an introverted character, not open to compromise and unaware of the unwritten laws that had to be followed in the relations with the media—found it hard to gain the trust and respect he deserved, on the part of the public and the press alike. "I had many problems, because I did not have any experiences I could put in my resume, and on top of that I was extremely shy," Francesco Bracali recalls.

Indeed, he still is the bashful type. Unlike most of his peers, he does not like the spotlight and the TV cameras: rather than speak in public, he would be in the kitchen. He is not and will never be a superstar, unlike those colleagues that ended up in TV shows and became well-known faces even among those who never set foot in one of their restaurants, and who probably never will.

I find it very hard to speak in public ... nowadays less than before, because life in its path puts you before much more serious and more difficult issues, so that at a certain point you end up giving things their right weight. So, if once speaking with a journalist seemed the hardest thing in the world, now I face these situations with a different approach. I tell myself that, however it goes, I know how to do my job. If I make a good impression, fine, otherwise, it'll be better next time.

Meanwhile, the restaurant's everyday routine, with its problems, tension, stress and arguments, was the territory where Francesco and Luca's relationship cemented. Their characters, so different yet complementary, often struck sparks when confronting.

One infamous occurrence was the Big T-Bone Incident, as Luca calls it with a big smile on his face. The reason that caused it? Who knows, so many years have passed. It started with an argument at work, like so many others. Francesco was slicing some T-Bone steaks, Luca was across the kitchen. The argument went on, tempers heated up, voices got altered, heavy words ensued. At a certain point Francesco lost his temper. He turned to Luca, steak in hand, and threw the piece of meat at him. Luca ducked down and avoided it by inches. Then the day went on, the brothers made peace, service at the restaurant continued as if nothing had happened. Late at night, before calling it a day, Luca stopped on the doorway, as if he remembered something. He called the cleaning lady: "Cesarina, please take that thing off the wall, will you?" Francesco had thrown the steak with such a strength, that it had remained stuck against the wall for hours.

Another consequence of the new course chosen by the two brothers was that now, at the restaurant tables, one could see more and more often a different kind of clientele: they ate alone, studied the menu attentively, spent quite some time perusing the wine list, observed the wine glasses, weighed the cutlery, asked questions that were not the usual small talk about the weather or the government typical of the average clientele. Francesco and Luca discovered two new types of guests: the educated gourmet, and the food guide inspector.

"The first time there came a gentleman from Rome, a certain Gigi De Santis, who wrote for *L'Espresso*. It was the end of the 1980s, when we were still undergoing the transition from *trattoria* to restaurant, but we were basically still the former. It was the first time someone ever wrote something about us," as Luca recalls.

Born in 1978, the restaurant guide published by *L'Espresso*—Italy's most popular weekly magazine with over 100,000 copies sold, published since 1955—was conceived as the Italian answer to the famous Gault-Millau guide, with votes expressed on a scale from 1 to 20, with 20 highest, based on the quality of food; the reviews included comments about service, price, the place's atmosphere, and a brief description of the menu. It was one of the first hints that Italy was starting to embrace the winds of change

Bracali and the Revolution in Tuscan Cuisine

of gastronomy: in France, *Nouvelle cuisine* was already a generally acknowledged concept, and the Gault-Millau guide had been its flagship.

"I still remember De Santis' phone call to book a table," Bracali continues.

> There were me and my dad, at the bar, tidying up after dinner service, and I immediately understood that the man must be a journalist. He did not drive a car, so we had to pick him up at the station in Follonica. At dinner, he was favorably impressed, and praised us a lot. He came back at lunch, the following day, and did not like it at all: he said that he had considered to take back everything he had written down the night before. You know why? Because of the flies. Swarms of flies. Back then, near the restaurant, there were a junkyard and a leather tanner, and in the summer it was a continuous battle with insects. They would fly into the restaurant all the time from the open porch, and we had to rely on bug sprays to chase them. But it was an unequal struggle. "Good thing for you I came to eat last night first," he said before leaving. "Or else..."

Then came the turn of *Gambero Rosso*. First published in December 1986, *Gambero Rosso* (Red Prawn) was at first an eight-page supplement of the self-titled "communist newspaper" *il manifesto*. Founded by Stefano Bonilli, and designed by the famed graphic artist Piergiorgio Maoloni, it represented another important step in the cultural revolution of food, firstly because it was born within the most politically committed of Italian newspapers: the creation of a supplement dedicated to food and wine marked the detachment from the common idea of pauperism within left-wing parties, and the acknowledgment that the pleasure of the senses through culinary and enogastronomic experience was no more a taboo for the Italian left. If, as the title of a famous 1971 film by Elio Petri ironically stated, *La classe operaia va in paradiso* (The Working Class Goes to Paradise), now it could be safely said that the working class could also be allowed to eat caviar and champagne. In 1987 *Gambero Rosso* evolved into a publishing company and published the first "Vini d'Italia" (Wines of Italy) guide, followed in 1990 by "Ristoranti d'Italia" (Restaurants of Italy) guide, which judged restaurants on a scale from 1 to 100. In 1992 there came a monthly magazine, also devoted to food and wine, with restaurants reviews, chefs' profiles, interviews.

"The first journalist from *Gambero Rosso* was Anna Moroni, who later became a popular TV personality when she took part in the program *La prova del cuoco* (The Cook's Challenge)." Based on the BBC format *Ready Steady Cook*, and broadcast daily from Monday to Friday at noon, *La prova del cuoco* is one of Italy's most popular TV programs on cuisine.

40

Then came other famous food journalists: Giancarlo Perrotta, Edoardo Raspelli, Luigi Cremona ... when a journalist comes to eat at a restaurant, you know it right away, even though some try to stay anonymous. It is more difficult to understand their feelings after a meal: there are those who seem satisfied, but then will write a harsh review, or dwell on negative details that take you by surprise. Others leave with a long face, but the following day they will write wonders about Bracali.

In 1994, with the help of Valeria Piccini and Gaetano Trovato, at just 23—two years younger than the minimum required by the statute—Francesco Bracali joined (or, in his words, "was pushed in") JRE Italia, the Italian branch of Jeunes Restaurateurs d'Europe, the association that brings together the most promising and talented young chefs from all over the Boot.

Since I first joined JRE until I came out of the association, the Tuscan members were all the same. It was a sort of closed circle. Those were the most beautiful years: unlike today, when it is all about innovation, and being the smartest, and having the highest rating on the guides, back then it could often happen that, after finishing service at four in the morning, we'd cook *spaghetti alla carbonara* for the crew and spend some time together in harmony and joy, with a team spirit that nowadays is no longer there. It was me, Valeria Piccini and Maurizio Menichetti, Gaetano Trovato, Susanna Fumi, who back then was the chef at the Vecchio Castello in Roccalbegna, and Marcello Crini, who now is at the Osteria di Passignano in Tavarnelle Val di Pesa and back then owned a restaurant near Florence, the Salotto del Chianti in Mercatale.

Together with Valeria and Maurizio, Francesco and Luca loved to go around and have dinner at their colleagues' restaurants. "Not to have fun and carouse, mind you. It was necessary to understand, to learn, to become experienced," as Luca points out.

Going out to dinner in an important restaurant meant taking good money out of our pockets and spending high sums. It was part of our work, and for a specific purpose: to try a great wine we were not familiar with, for instance. And in order to drink certain bottles you needed to spend quite a lot of money, and make sacrifices. To learn about wine you have to taste a lot of it. Nobody is born with the knowledge of it.

After joining JRE Italy, the name Bracali started to become known among food and wine enthusiasts and gourmets. To many, he was the next big thing in the world of fine dining, and as it often happens, word of mouth raised lots of interest and curiosity.

"I was still the talented kid who needed to be 'tested.' But we were young, and enthusiastic. We felt that the future could be ours, and no one could stop us. And then..."

The Accident

Four a.m., on a Saturday night in June 1995.

Francesco had just returned home after a night at the disco with his friends. He liked music, loved dancing, and often stayed out all night long. He often hung around places where drugs were liberally consumed, but the idea of using never even crossed his mind. He liked the adrenaline of music, the pumping bass that shakes the bowels, the spellbinding rhythm that conquers you and makes you move in unison with everyone else; but at the same time he wanted to remain always fully conscious. He wanted to stay in control. And, on top of that, he would never betray his parents' trust.

That night Luca was out of town too. He was late, more than usual, and was driving back to Massa Marittima, after driving home his fiancée Tania. He and Francesco drove two Lancia Delta cars. Both gray, almost identical. Both brothers liked speed and fast cars, as well as the feeling of pushing on the accelerator pedal, and Luca was especially enthusiastic about motors, engines, rallies.

Francesco arrived in Massa Marittima with a friend, and stopped at a parking lot a few steps from home, to smoke one more cigarette and chat a little bit. It was a quiet night, one of those late spring nights where the fresh night air fills the lungs and already smells of summer.

"At a certain point I decided to go. It was already four o'clock and I had to wake up early. Several minutes later, a friend of mine passed by and told my friend that "Bracalino," as they used to call me, had had a serious car accident. My friend said it was impossible, because I was here with him just a few minutes earlier, but the other insisted ... and then they both realized that Luca's car was nearly identical to mine."

On his way back to Massa Marittima, Luca felt the fatigue weigh on his eyelids. He was just a couple of miles from home, but his eyes kept closing all the time. Better to stop for a moment, and take a breath of fresh air. It was a beautiful night, full of stars. Luca slowed down and stopped the car in a little pitch just out of town. There was a Carabinieri patrol car there, on the lookout during the usual night shift. Familiar faces: everybody knows everyone else in a little village, and Luca was a well-known one, even though his restaurant was still seen by many like some sort of an exotic animal. Luca got out of the car, stretched his legs, had a small talk with the two police officers. They offered to accompany him home:

their shift had just ended, and it was time for them to go home too. The two cars drove away from the pitch, Luca's Lancia Delta ahead, the Carabinieri's Alfa Romeo Giulietta behind.

At a certain point, the two officers noticed that that the other car was accelerating sharply in the straight road that leads to Massa Marittima, before the ascent to the village. Seventy-five miles an hour. Eighty-five. Hundred. Hundred-and-ten.... At first the two policemen thought Luca was playing a practical joke on them, but the Lancia Delta did not slow down. There must be something wrong. The police car honked, flashed, tried to reach it. But there was nothing they could do: Luca had fallen asleep, with his foot pressed on the accelerator. And his car drove faster and faster, toward its destiny.

The race was stopped by an acacia tree on the roadside, the last one at the end of the straight. The Lancia Delta crashed against it at such a speed that the tree was literally eradicated. To this day, Francesco still wonders whether that tree was deleterious or providential: without that acacia, Luca's Lancia would have ended in a field. Maybe it would have overturned, with lethal consequences for its driver, maybe not ... maybe, maybe...

Francesco's friend ran under Bracali's house—back then Francesco lived with his grandparents and took care of his invalid maternal grandfather—and asked him to come down on a pretext, telling him of an argument between two acquaintances which he must discuss. Francesco realized that something was wrong, but did not think it had anything to do with Luca: as far as he knew, at that hour of the night his older brother had been sleeping in bed for a while. They joined a group of friends, who had already learned of the accident, so as to get more news about what happened, then headed to the house of Francesco's parents. As soon as they left, though, they came across an ambulance driving at full speed with sirens wailing in the opposite direction, and followed it to the emergency room. Francesco recalls,

> At the hospital, my brother's body was completely covered by blankets, and I could only see his face. So, I did not understand the seriousness of the situation immediately. I realized it was quite serious, because of all the blood transfusions and emergency procedures that were going on around him. Then a helicopter was requested to take him to the better equipped Grosseto hospital, 30 miles away.

Luca was hospitalized in the intensive care unit at the Grosseto hospital, in critical condition. Then he was moved to Pisa, where he underwent no less than fifteen surgeries, necessary to remedy the thirty-two different fractures in his lower limbs. His right ankle and elbow had been virtually destroyed. What is more, only in Pisa the doctors diagnosed a fracture at the second cervical vertebra: in Grosseto his head had been moved when the medical team cut his hair to get stitches on his scalp, and Luca had been in danger of remaining quadriplegic. To avoid irreparable damage to the spine, he was applied a sort of helmet, with two screws planted in the skull, which did not allow any neck movement.

Rehabilitation was long and painful, and at first it looked like a mirage. At that time, tutors were not a widespread tool: doctors resorted to plaster casts, which forced the patient to absolute immobility. On top of that, to make up for bone calcifications, it was necessary to resort to the release under anesthesia of the elbow, knee and ankle: the last resort to recover the functionality of the limbs.

"One day Luca had a really serious breakdown, " Francesco recalls. "He could not take it anymore, and kept repeating that he just wanted to leave the hospital. My father was desperate, because at that time the only part of his body which Luca could move was his left arm, and dad did not know where to take him." What to do, then? Luciano and Francesco asked around and found out about a neurocognitive rehabilitation center in Northern Italy, in Schio, near Vicenza. It was headed by the eminent neurologist Professor Carlo Perfetti, the inventor of the "Perfetti method," also known as Cognitive Therapeutic Exercise, a rehabilitation system for hemiplegic patients who had suffered a stroke. At the cost of further economic sacrifices, including the sale of the family house, they collected enough money for a visit. After visiting Luca, who could barely move his left arm, Perfetti was adamant that a further surgical treatment was absolutely necessary in addition to rehabilitation, and recommended Bracali to entrust to his colleague, Professor Livio Nogarin, chief of the orthopedic trauma department in Vicenza.

"When professor Nogarin first looked at Luca's radiographs," Francesco recalls, "he told me: 'I have already seen this patient!' It turned out that he had examined those radiographs during a convention in Vienna, when my brother's situation had been brought up as a case example by a professor in Pisa who was treating him." A very direct and frank relationship was established between the doctor and the patient: Nogarin told Luca that, if he wanted to be cured, he had to trust him blindly, and submit to the entire surgery program that the professor had envisioned for him, from beginning to end. It would be a long and difficult path, but a necessary one. Otherwise, the professor would never consider such a complex case, and of such gravity.

Luca Bracali remained hospitalized in Schio for eight months; at regular intervals he was taken to the Vicenza or Verona hospital, and underwent surgery at the hands of Professor Nogarin: fifteen more interventions overall. Rehab was long and tiring, through thick and thin: once the fixers were removed from the legs, the doctors found out that the bones had not calcified properly, and plastered the patient back from neck to toe. Luca's mother was constantly at his side, while Francesco came and went from the hospital to the restaurant, and vice versa.

"My life was like that," Francesco remembers.

> I took the bus at four in the morning, with the commuters who went to work at the Piombino steelworks. Then I waited at the Follonica station for the 7 a.m. train, and after several changes I arrived at the hospital at 3 in the afternoon. I stayed there all day and went back to the restaurant on the following day with my father, by car. This, if surgery had gone well. If it hadn't, I closed the restaurant and went back to Schio. There was a time when Luca was plastered all over again, and we were all staying around him. Such situations, either they completely destroy a family, or they tie you together in binds that are stronger than anything in the world, and will stay like that until you die. There is no middle ground.

It was a dramatic period for the Bracali family, and not just because of Luca's car accident. To Francesco, there came the time of a real, harsh confrontation with Luciano. Bracali's relationship with his dad had been difficult and often stormy, and when father and son found themselves alone in the restaurant, having to manage it all by themselves while Luciano was at Luca's bedside, it resulted in chickens coming home to roost.

> One day there was this huge, furious quarrel. We almost came to blows. And when you are almost coming to blows with a parent, it is a point of no return. These are moments that mark you forever. And, well, on that occasion something clicked. My father burst out in tears. It was the first time I saw him cry in my life. From that moment on, our relationship was welded again, and even became stronger than ever. Not quiet, no. We would still have arguments in the future. But my inner rage, the rage that had led me to run away from home at fourteen, had faded at last.

Luca came back to work at the restaurant at the end of 1997. Nearly three years had gone by. Three years of surgeries, hospitalizations, painful rehabilitation, economic sacrifices. For the first weeks, he served wine and dishes while leaning on tripods.

It was a new beginning, or rather, a new challenge. Then came the first proper renovation works on the restaurant: the open porch—previously a simple canopy under which people could eat outside during the summer, with an ice cream freezer in sight—was closed and turned into a small room.

Back on their feet, the Bracali family started to walk again, but in their minds they were ready to run, for a race that had been abruptly interrupted three years earlier.

Starlight

The interview in the March 1997 issue of *La Cucina Italiana*, with Toni Cuman's off-the-record prophecy on the restaurant's forthcoming closure, was yet another bitter pill to swallow. On the other hand, the presence in such a prestigious magazine was still a flagship to be proud of for the 26-year-old chef. However, the dishes illustrated in the article were somewhat misleading for those who were not familiar with Bracali's conception of *haute cuisine*: a minimalistic leek pudding with Parmesan cheese sauce; an artichoke *lasagna* with sweetbreads which recalled the style of Gualtiero Marchesi's open ravioli; a lamb fillet in a crust of aromatic herbs with zucchini, carrots and onions; and, to conclude, a hypercaloric citrus terrine with hazelnut pralines which looked unmistakably very 1990s.

"That was not 'my' style of cooking," Bracali explains.

That article was done "on request," and the dishes were considerably simpler than the menu I was offering at the restaurant, which on the contrary was far too rich and creative, even overloaded with ingredients. What is more, that *lasagna* was clearly inspired by Marchesi. I was young and inexperienced, and it showed. And when the moment came of preparing my dishes so that pictures would be taken of them, I realized the difference from my experience in Ghirlanda: when I prepared the dessert, the journalist did not ask me questions on the technique I employed for the terrine, but he wanted to know about its caloric content. Something which I had never thought of.

In Milan—the city of fashion, populated by adherents to the cult of the body—calories were a matter of primary importance. And Francesco's dessert, with its heavy butter content, was perceived as something unthinkable. Whereas Bracali, who had grown up as a kid with his grandmother's pies and desserts cooked in the oven, had never considered calories as an issue. He realized that he had to reconsider many of his recipes under this new light, to make them lighter and more digestible.

And yet, after so many tribulations, 1997 ended under an auspicious light. Together with Moreno Cedroni, the brilliant chef of the two-star Madonnina del Pescatore in Marzocca di Senigallia, and other colleagues of JRE—Valeria Piccini, Claudio Sadler, Alessandra Buriani, Karl Baumgartner—Francesco participated in a Christmas special issue of the *Gambero Rosso* magazine (*"A tavola con babbochef,"* December 1997). He introduced a new recipe, a two-color Savarin cake with sole and vegetables and a fish soup, inspired by a traditional recipe, the red mullet Livorno-style. Despite his shyness, the young chef even appeared in the photo shoot that adorned the magazine cover, in which the participants posed dressed as Father Christmas: Cedroni with a phony long white beard, Valeria wearing the red and white jacket, and so on. Francesco was portrayed with the bag of gifts over his shoulder, with the hope that the new year would bring him and his family a little bit of luck and serenity.

With Luca's return the restaurant started to run at full speed again, and the results were not long in coming. In 1999 the *Gambero Rosso* guide awarded Bracali with seven points more than the previous year, from 78 to 85. An acceleration that took Francesco's breath away. It was not the only time this would occur during that magic year.

Around the same time, a new presence showed up at the restaurant, one that would also take an important place in Francesco Bracali's life. One day, a young blonde girl, very pretty, came to lunch with her former employer, the owner of an important eatery in Montecatini. Her name was Nadia Frosini. Born in Pistoia, she had taken the trip to Massa Marittima in the hopes of a training experience at Bracali's restaurant. She would soon become a member of the dining room staff: good-looking, elegant, smart, with a strong character, she had the grace and the verve that made her the perfect complement to Luca.

At the beginning, though, Francesco and Nadia strongly disliked each other. She was very direct in her opinions, and diplomacy was not one of her best qualities. If something was wrong with the kitchen, the service, the management, she would stand up and say it straight in Francesco and Luca's face. Then things changed. "My father and my mother liked Nadia immediately. He always told me: look, this girl is mad as a hatter, but she's one of a kind. You will never find anyone like her anymore." Between Nadia and Francesco a deep feeling was born, a working relationship and a love story that lasted eleven years. "I don't know if that was a sign of destiny, but I like to think so: that day Nadia first came to lunch, a fax arrived: the Michelin Guide had awarded the restaurant with the Michelin star for the year 1999/2000. I was the youngest chef in Europe to have achieved that goal."

The annually published Michelin Red Guide is the oldest European hotel and restaurant reference guide. It was born in 1900, when tire manufacturers André and Édouard Michelin decided to publish a traveling companion for motorists, to give away for free, in order to boost the demand for cars (and, of course, for car tires). It included information for those who traveled by car: maps, lists of mechanics, petrol stations, but also hotels and inns. Other guides followed, for other countries (Belgium, the Alps region, German, Spain, the British Isles, etcetera), but it was not until 1926 that the Michelin Guide introduced its star award system. Initially, only one star was awarded to the best fine dining establishments, but starting in 1931 a new hierarchic system of awards, with a range from zero to three stars, made its debut. The criteria for the starred rankings were published in 1936, and were as follows: One star meant "A very good restaurant in its category"; two stars meant "Excellent cooking, worth a detour"; and three meant "Exceptional cuisine, worth a special journey." Michelin reviewers are called "inspectors" and they are anonymous figures: this means that they do not identify themselves to the chefs and owners, and behave like ordinary guests; this is to maintain an objective judgment of the dining experience. Their expenses are paid by the Michelin company.

Compared to the French Michelin Guide, the Italian one has always featured a much lesser number of starred restaurants, and earning even one star meant a boost not only in prestige but also, more pragmatically, in the economy of the restaurant itself, for the guide itself is nothing short of a bible for fine dining lovers, not just Italian but foreign as well, and thus it dramatically enhances the income. Earning a Michelin star meant that the transformation had been completed. The Bracali restaurant was now an internationally recognized fine dining establishment.

To Francesco it was a dream come true. The award ceremony took place in London, and he arrived in United Kingdom accompanied by Valeria Piccini, whose restaurant had just been awarded with two Michelin stars. The prize was handed to him by none other than Paul Bocuse, the

"Pope" of French gastronomy, the father of Nouvelle cuisine, awarded with three Michelin stars since 1965 and honored as the "Chef of the Century" at the Culinary Institute of America in 2011. Bocuse (1926–2018) was— and still is—an institution in France, to the point that he was the first chef to have his own statue at the Paris Wax Museum. Bracali still recalls the award ceremony with affection: "We were staying at a hotel near London Bridge, and I remember I was given a beautiful suite. It was like a dream. To Bocuse it was just routine, and I was just one of many, but to me it was a real honor to receive that award from his hands."

However, all this—the leap forward in the *Gambero Rosso* guide, the first Michelin star—was not something Francesco was fully prepared to deal with. And in hindsight he himself admitted it. "I lived those things as a kid. I was absolutely not ready for all that, I did not catch the moment and I did not have around me people who could have helped me along this path, perhaps in a more detached way, but more rational and constructive. More focused, in short. In my career—or rather, since I don't like the term 'career,' I would say in my personal journey—I have always suffered for not having a family which could recognize certain flaws in my style and help me improve upon then, as it was the case with, say, Massimiliano Alajmo, the chef owner of the three-Michelin-stars Le Calandre, in Rubano, near Padua. The Alajmo family is the emblem of professionalism: Massimiliano is a culinary genius, and he became the youngest chef in Europe to have ever been awarded three stars from the Michelin guide, but part of the credit in his professional and personal growth must be given to his family. In my case, such a thing could not happen, since we had no specific background in the world of *haute cuisine*. Therefore, to my father, one day I was the greatest chef in Italy, nothing short of a genius whom he would carry in the palm of his hand. But if the next day, say, a guest would complain about a dish, or the bank would call him because there were bills to pay, he started again to have doubts, and say that maybe we were doing all wrong. The inexperience was mine as well as theirs: we were all starting from scratch."

Such an immaturity had severe consequences in personal relationships, and Bracali's impulsiveness led him to leave JRE. Nevertheless, the relationship with Nadia gave Francesco a greater confidence in his own professional skills, and pushed him to commit, experiment, dare even more. His dishes became more complex, the number of ingredients increased, their concepts relied on contrasts and juxtapositions, on unusual pairings, on the combination of different temperatures and opposing textures.

In November 2000, food journalist Salvatore Marchese celebrated Francesco Bracali, labeling him "The Miracle of Maremma," as Chef of the month in the magazine *Fuoricasa*. Curly hair, barely noticeable goatee, Bracali smiles bashfully to the camera, while the article underlines the "appealing balance between *auteur* cuisine and family warmth, quality of the service and friendly atmosphere" of the restaurant. The latter was the effect of the staff being an enlarged family of sorts, with Luciano, Luca and Nadia serving the guests in the dining room: it was easy for guests to become acquainted with the personnel, and developing a more strict relationship that could turn into a real friendship. Such was the case of the German-born Frank Nickel. Frank and his wife visit Italy at least once or twice a year, preferably Tuscany, and became regulars at Bracali's table since the very first steps of its transformation into a fine dining establishment. Over time, a friendship was born, and Luca agreed to take them to various tasting tours in Italy's most prestigious wineries, not only in Tuscany but also in Lombardy, Piedmont, Marche.... With such guests as Frank, Luciano would be more relaxed and at ease, but he also felt even more responsible for the food that was served, and tried to give them the best he could, making them taste unique delicacies—some particular type of cheese, for instance.

One evening, near the end of the meal, he wanted to impress Frank and his party with an extraordinary taleggio cheese he had just purchased from a small farmer, enclosed in its typical wooden box. Taleggio is a semi-soft cheese, smear-ripened, and with a very strong smell, produced since Roman times. It is delicious, but it must be consumed quickly as it tends to melt at room temperature; for this reason, it is often used in *risotto* or on *polenta*. Luciano started composing the cheese plate, placing bites of different types accompanied with homemade jams. Then came the turn of the taleggio: he opened the box and.... Frank and the other guests could distinctly hear a desperate cry of distress, followed—in typical Tuscan fashion—by a series of curses and barely suffocated swearings. The taleggio had completely melted inside the box. A more experienced restaurateur would have probably kept his mouth shut and served something else instead, but Luciano was just too disappointed. And, as Tuscan people do, he expressed his disappointment in unmistakable fashion. Unprofessional? Maybe. Sincere? Absolutely. He apologized: "I cannot offer you this cheese anymore—it does not look good!" Frank and his companions asked to taste it nevertheless. "And to this day I have never tasted a better taleggio," he recalls.

In that period, those who sat at one of the tables in Ghirlanda to try Francesco's dishes could choose among such baroque creations as the following: Turbot fillet in a crust of orange-perfumed bread, served with a warm fennel-and-leek salad, raw oranges and vinaigrette; chickpeas soup with a cauliflower, lentils and sautéed raisins gateau, and crispy prawns in *lardo di Colonnata*; two-color *lasagna* stuffed with scallops, mussels and clams with a cream of potato and lettuce, a sauce of scallops coral, *filangé* potatoes and fried sage; pasta ravioli with breadcrumbs, sautéed with roast gravy, pumpkin cream and chives; pigeon breast with porcini mushrooms on vine leaves.

Meanwhile the restaurant kept growing and shedding skin. The name Bracali was increasingly present on the lips of gourmets and food experts and in the guides. But it also turned up in those websites, forums, blogs and newsgroups which were increasingly becoming a new reference for lovers of gastronomy and *haute cuisine*. Such an evolution found Bracali still unprepared.

> It was quite a complicated moment, because the more the media attention grew, the more I should have taken advantage of certain situations and opportunities. Which I did not do, partly because of my character, and partly because I had no one behind me who encouraged me and drove me in a certain way. I was still the talented young chef, but in Italy there were many others coming out in the spotlight. So, this became a period of constant growth and challenge, study and continuous testings, of comparison with my colleagues and with myself as well.

In the first years of the new millennium, Bracali offered an array of dishes characterized by an engaging creativity, in which typical Tuscan ingredients were revisited and transformed, sometimes provocatively. That was the case with the Cinta Senese salami soup. Cinta Senese is a breed of domestic pig from the province of Siena, one of the six autochthonous pig breeds in Italy, and it owes its name to its black coat with a white sash (called *cinta*) which runs across its shoulders, sides and front legs. The breed is native to the region of Tuscany, and has been known since the middle ages: a Cinta pig is depicted in the fresco painted in 1337 by Ambrogio Lorenzetti in the Palazzo Comunale in Siena's Piazza del Campo. A popular farm animal, with sturdy limbs, long ears and a long snout with a thick grout that allows it to dig in the dirt, it gradually diminished over the centuries and was included in the list of endangered species in the 1990s, before it was rediscovered and made popular again by gastronomy, which resulted in it being awarded the DOP certification from the European Community. Cinta Senese pigs are raised free range, and fed with natural grazing and pelleted non–GM cereals, and result in high quality products, such as salami, sausages, capocollo, cured lard, pork loin, and prosciutto (ham).

Another dish—small fried ravioli with buffalo mozzarella, shallots and Prato mortadella, in a rhubarb and marjoram sauce, created in 2003— underlined the essence of opulence and abundance of Francesco's creations, which ran counter to the tendency of Italian cuisine of the period, characterized by a more and more minimalistic conception and execution.

Whereas my dishes were quite the opposite: stuffed with elements, full of ingredients and daring combinations, opulent. Even too much. Frankly, I tended to exaggerate. I was fascinated by excess, by the idea of overcoming myself. In each dish there were a number of things that to me seemed to work, but which in fact were missing something fundamental, something which nowadays, with experience and professional maturity, I have understood. One thing is to have a very good intuition to start with, another thing is to create a dish that is fully balanced and complete in itself. And in my dishes, back then, there was an excess brought by my own inexperience. An excess for which in the following years I paid the price abundantly. It took me a lot of time to regain the trust of the press and the media.

In 2003—the year the *L'Espresso* guide awarded Bracali with a score of 16/20, while Gambero Rosso awarded the restaurant with 89/100, just one step below 90/100, which meant the prestigious *"tre forchette"* (three forks) award to the country's very best restaurants—the tasting menu was emblematic in this sense:

- Hot caramelized eggplant balls, filled with parmesan cheese ice cream wrapped in smoked jelly, on a bed of potato foam;
- Eggplant rolls stuffed with langoustines and Buffalo mozzarella on a basil sauce, confit tripe and a Bavarian cake of *pappa al pomodoro*;
- Octopus-and-beans flan in a soup of shallots and crushed grapes, with julienne cucumbers;
- Green spaghetti with gurnard and chives on a sauce of caramelized celery and sausage, and candied tomatoes;
- Garlic-flavored pigeon lasagna with a veil of foie gras in a cold melon sauce and salad in vinaigrette;

- Variation of fish and lupin beans: salmon egg tart with lobster and lupin beans mousse, caramelized Grana cheese and red wine sauce; vacuum cooked sea bream fillet with honey and thyme, arugula sauce, lupin beans with Balsamic vinegar and julienne of Cinta Senese prosciutto; warm lupin beans and octopus salad with tomato, Taggiasca olives, and fried onion rings;
- Ricotta gateau on a celery and apple sauce with tomato sorbet.

The sheer amount of ingredients is mind-numbing. Each dish looks like a combination of three or four different dishes, blended together by a crazed sorcerer's apprentice: for instance, Bracali's love for surprising textures is manifest in such elements as the Parmesan ice cream or the tomato sorbet.

The reinvention of traditional Tuscan recipes is another constant: for instance, *pappa al pomodoro* (tomato pap) is a typical tomato and bread soup, the remnant of the rural habit of making the best out of poor ingredients. Stale bread, too hard and no longer good to eat, is doused with water, squeezed and added to a tomato soup (cooked with red pepper flakes, onion, garlic, oil, salt and pepper), then stirred and mashed so as to obtains a porridge-like, very thick soup, which is served with the addition of olive oil and garnished with basil leaves: a phenomenal delicacy. In Bracali's version it turned into a savory cake, and becomes a side element of a dish centered on eggplant and mozzarella, which on the one hand recalls another typical Italian recipe, *melanzane alla parmigiana*, and on the other adds such elements as the langoustine and the veal tripe. It is a rollercoaster ride for the taste buds.

The attention to the raw material is also evident in the choice of such ingredients as the Taggiasca olives, a small and particularly tasty variety from the nearby region of Liguria, and the lupin beans, the yellow legume seeds which retain a rather bitter taste unless properly rinsed, and which were (and still are) very hard to find in *haute cuisine* recipes. The lupin beans dish was a virtuoso concept, offering a variation of such an unusual element: in Francesco's idea, it was like offering various arrangements and mixes of the same song, proving that the same ingredient can develop into many and often surprising ways.

By the end of 2004 Francesco and Luca decided that it was time to give the restaurant a proper restyling. To rethink and redesign the interiors—the hall, the dining room, the kitchen, the lounge where guests would taste spirits and cigars next to a fireplace—and create an environment that would reflect not only the idea of cuisine that they offered, but especially their aesthetic taste. A place to match their ambitions, where the beauty and taste of the dishes are enhanced and complemented by the sight that is presented to diners when they look up from their plates.

An emblematic choice, in this sense, was the open kitchen (by De Manincor) equipped with all the most advanced accessories, including a Roner for low-temperature cooking, an Irinox blast chiller, a Pacojet, a vacuum packaging machine, and separated from the dining room by a large glass framed like a painting. A choice in the vein of Marchesi and Vissani, whose restaurants both featured (among the very first in Italy) similar open kitchens. But it was not a stunt *à la manière de...*: the concept of painting, of creation, of framing, has always been fundamental in Francesco Bracali's work. Every dish starts firstly with the knowledge of its own limits and boundaries, and its placement in the circular, immaculate space of the porcelain that receives it, and takes life as a sketch where the shape and the basic elements are outlined.

But the frame, in a broader sense, is all that comes around the sensory experience of food, and which inevitably brings to it, inside the restaurant. To make just an example, that is the case of the sorbets cart, designed by Francesco himself: an idea that went against the guidelines in the restaurant world, and which brought back childhood memories, for a moment that marks a passage from the salty part of the meal to the desserts. "It's one of those things which guests or journalists appreciated more with time, than in the moment they were introduced," Luca observes. In fact, such an accessory caused controversy and perplexities at first, but the concept eventually proved winning: the presentation aimed at evoking childhood days, namely the image of ice cream vendors at a time when ice-creams and sorbets were not in plain sight, and the various tastes were a mystery hidden underneath those steel covers. A return to the past reminiscent of the epiphany experienced by food critic Anton Ego in the movie *Ratatouille* (2007). Finally, the concept of frame worked as a boundary, a point of separation and the sign of identity and uniqueness of a microcosm—indeed, a whole world, as in *mondobracali* (Bracaliworld), the website that would mark Luca and Francesco's appearance on the web a few years later.

It was a bold and challenging project, not only economically. After four months' work, what was born as a village *trattoria* reopened to the public in April 2005 with a completely new look. At first glance, on the outside, it might seem that very little had changed, in the house in Via Perolla, at the junction with the road that leads to Massa Marittima: perhaps only the perfectly cured miniature garden, in the small sidewalk in front of the entrance, which softened the exterior appearance. But once walked past the door, one would find an environment worthy of the great French *maisons*, with wood parquers, columns and Versace vases.

The Calabrese designer's Greek key emblem was the recurring motif of the ceramics and sets of dishes—the Barocco, Les Trésors de la mer, Le Jardin de Versace, porcelains which today are no longer available on the market, and were sought after and collected with care and stubbornness by Francesco—with the black and gold combination standing out amid the luminous white of the rooms. A courageous, strong choice, which stood in contrast with the minimal-chic dictates that characterized many *haute cuisine* Italian restaurants. Once again, the driving key was the concept of frame as a complement and a necessary tinsel of artistic creation. As Bracali explained,

> I wanted something that would remain in time: something classical, with character, which would reflect me for what I am and which would never tire me first, since in the end it is I who have to work at the restaurant for 20 hours a day. As a fashion enthusiast, I always had a soft spot for Versace, because for inspiration he looked back to historic elements, to Ancient Greece. His was not just a beautiful logo, but a historical relic, which had been passed along for thousands of years. His creations, his dresses, his design objects are always steeped in history and ancient culture. And I love Versace also because he was one of the first designers to have created accessories specifically for the table: I wanted something that would "speak" of history and Italian spirit. Some people label him as 'heavy' and opulent, which somehow bothers me. Unlike other fashion designers, Versace managed to make even opulence elegant.

Elegance in opulence is a definition which fit perfectly Bracali's now mature style. He managed to turn even poor food such as anchovies and sardines into something rich and elegant, in such masterful dishes as the dome of tomato and eggplant on a tart of anchovies, burrata cream and tomato water, or the seared and marinated bonito with Jerusalem artichoke cream, light coffee meringue and extra virgin olive oil ice cream.

This opulence was to be enriched even more over the years with further details, as with regards to the "frame." Perhaps these choices were difficult to understand at first, for an outsider; however, they underline why to the Bracali brothers the concept of restaurant goes beyond the mere economic activity linked to food and wine. For example, the beautiful original tiles designed by Piero Fornasetti, displayed on the kitchen wall, and which the majority of the diners will never even glimpse. But which *must* be there, those and not any other, there and not anywhere else. Fornasetti (1919–1988) was a famed painter, sculptor, interior decorator and engraver whose style had been profoundly influenced by the Greek and Roman architecture, and who made a heavy use of black and white. Francesco recalls,

> I first saw his works in Milan, many years ago, exposed in a small shop, even before we redesigned the restaurant, and I just fell in love with his style right away. I came across Fornasetti's creations years later, by sheer chance. For the dining room, I had played on the black and gold combination, as a reference to Versace, whereas for the kitchen I wanted a very technical look, a combination of black and steel, with the De Manincor stove at the center. One day I went to a showroom in Grosseto, to purchase some tiles designed by Laura Biagiotti for the dining room floor, and I noticed a whole display of Fornasetti tiles. I did not hesitate for a moment, even though they cost a fortune. But I immediately decided that I wanted them in my kitchen.

Francesco Bracali in his kitchen next to the tiles designed by Piero Fornasetti.

Another addition was the cheese trolley, in cherry and black wood, designed by Bracali himself and built by a wood artisan in Pistoia, Yari Fanti. It was another accessory that cost several thousand euros: rationally, an excessive outlay, since in the economy of a restaurant the cheese course is very often a surplus, a luxury which is hard to maintain and often means a loss in the budget: to keep "alive" a cheese cart implies high costs, because the products have a very short life; they often have to be thrown away and replaced before their inevitable decay, and the profits are laughable. To Bracali, then, the cheese cart was not merely eye candy for the guests, but much more: yet another sign of identity. It was an accessory turned into an *objet d'art*, a unique and inimitable piece. Because that cheese trolley—elegant, unmistakable, stylish—can be found only there, in Ghirlanda, near Massa Marittima. The same can be said about the wooden ham carrier, the bottle holders, the wooden *tableau* on which the *entrées* are served, and so on.

As the great director Marco Ferreri loved to say, for a true filmmaker there is one and only one way to film a scene. In Bracali's concept, every detail, even the most infinitesimal, had to have its own specific purpose—either aesthetic, symbolic or logical. Just like a piece of a mosaic, or a paint stroke that gives yet another nuance to a painting, or a chiseling that defines a form, a face, an expression which to a casual observer would already seem perfect, but which to the artist's eye is necessary to achieve the desired result. "Francesco understands immediately when a thing is beautiful. He 'feels' its strength at once, he realizes the aesthetic concept behind a work of art at first sight," Luca explains. "It is something innate." Inevitably, these aesthetic choices were destined to raise perplexities, misunderstandings, criticism; but over the years they have proved unassailable by time. Indelible. Neither trendy nor pandering, but, quite simply, beautiful.

The wine cellar grew as well: the 700 wine labels Luca had collected in 1997, ten years later had become 17,000; that is, about 20,000 bottles with an annual rotation of 5,000 pieces. A cellar with a strong personality, assembled over time through important decisions, with the enhancement of small labels and producers, in order to offer a unique choice of products. "The wine list has changed a lot over the years," Luca recalls. "At the beginning, when we started, there was the desire—wrong, and costly too—to have everything, and immediately. To have what all the others had: prestigious labels, great vintage wines. At the beginning, I followed Maurizio

Menichetti, and his choices, like a shadow. Whatever Maurizio purchased, to me it was the Gospel." Then, little by little, Luca started walking with his own legs, and followed his own ideas about wine.

> I have three rules when purchasing wine today. The first: go for the real great wines in the world. However, whatever people may say, there are few really "great" wines—those with a great longevity, which acquire complexity, balance and elegance over time, and with a strong link with the territory. And yet, in the world of wine, thanks to the media, for years and years labels have been sponsored, and producers and wines have been magnified way beyond their merits. They were good, sometimes very good wines, sure. But not top-notch. Not "great" wines. Second: get to know the winery—who manages it, how it works. I always tried to meet the producer, to know him personally. To me, it is fundamental: I never buy a wine blindly. Neither in Italy, nor in Europe. It is important to have a relationship with the producer, to nurture a friendship, to confront our ideas and visions. Third, and most important, love the wine: if I don't like what I taste, there is no friendship this can withstand, not even with local producers. To me, it would be unthinkable to suggest that wine to the restaurant guests, it is stronger than me. However, to many this would be considered a fault, as there are some wines that sell a lot because they are fashionable, for they have a taste that can please many. But if I am not convinced, no way.

On the Way to the Second Star

The butterfly finally left the cocoon: a great restaurant was born in Ghirlanda, Tuscany. Food magazines realized it, and their correspondents started to show up more and more often at Bracali's door.

Francesco Bracali ended up on the cover of *I Grandi Vini* (July/August 2005), which dedicated a long article to "Maremma, an area of gastronomic excellence." One month later he participated in a special issue of *Cucina & Vini* (September 2005), where he spoke at length about his Tuscan roots, in contraposition with the Far East sirens that lured many of his colleagues: "I am determined not to follow the fashion of the moment, that has everyone looking at the Orient. I prefer to maintain the strong roots that bind me to my native territory."

Then came the turn of the classy *Monsieur* magazine, which in November 2006 reunited four major Tuscan chefs: Francesco Bracali, Gaetano Trovato, Andrea Mazzone (of the Rossini restaurant in Florence) and the legendary Fulvio Pierangelini, whose two-star Michelin restaurant Gambero Rosso in San Vincenzo, a small fishing village on the Tirrenian sea opened in 1980, was considered by many Italy's very best, and was voted 12th best in the world in 2008's Restaurant Top 50. The article, bearing the cinephile title *Il ritorno dell'oca selvaggia* ("The Return of the Wild Geese"), followed the four chefs as they prepared four different game dishes in a restaurant in San Gimignano, one of the most beautiful villages in Tuscany. It was a prestigious occurrence, which signaled that Bracali was by then considered one of the top-notch names in Italian cuisine.

On the occasion, Francesco chose to prepare a pasta dish—hare ravioli with hare gravy, celeriac purée and rhubarb compote—where he played in his own way and with a mature hand with the juxtaposition of sweet and sour, with the smell of smoke and the intriguing intensity of rhubarb. Even more significant is the opening photo: the charismatic Pierangelini dominates the shot, at the center, whereas on its right, the boyish smile and narrow eyes of young Bracali stand out. He looks like a child in a candy store, enjoying every minute of it. The context was the right one: *Monsieur* was a magazine dedicated to the *bon vivre* in all its aspects, from *haute couture* clothes to watches, from cars to jewels, from cigars to fine dining. A concept in tune with the one that pushed the young chef to chisel, piece by piece, detail after detail, his cuisine and his restaurant.

That same month, an article in the *Gambero Rosso* magazine reported about a lecture given by Bracali at Rome's *Città del Gusto* (City of Taste), an architectural complex inaugurated in October 2002 that comprised TV studies, professional schools, a wine bar, a restaurant and a pizzeria, as well as a *"teatro della cucina"* (kitchen theater) where mundane events related to gastronomy were held. In many ways, the Città del Gusto was the emblem of the now widespread appeal of *haute cuisine* among the Italian public: three years earlier, in 1999, *Gambero Rosso* had inaugurated its own TV channel, dedicated exclusively to food and wine. Whereas previously gastronomy on television had been a matter of simple cooking lessons and the like, the audience showed a growing interest in fine dining and drinking, and the country's most important chefs started to become household faces and names. Lecturing at the Città del Gusto meant being part of an elitist, selected group; to Francesco, who had retired from school because he could not stand his professors, being on the other side of the fence meant a symbolic revenge, and more. It meant having become a teacher—having precious knowledge to share and pass on to others.

As his professional self-confidence increased, Francesco became more at ease and eclectic, both in his personality and in his look. In the *Gambero Rosso* photo shoot, the chef displays a canary blond hair which almost steals the show. The dishes he presented were all centered around the porcini mushroom. First, a guinea fowl tart with vegetables, porcini on wine leaves and chestnut sauce, where the vehemence of the mushroom was balanced by the sweetness of the autumnal fruit, while the vegetable topping enhanced the taste of the guinea fowl. Then, *casarecci* (a Sicilian variety of pasta: narrow, thin, twisted and rolled tubes about 2 inches long, made from semolina) with lobster and porcini in a sauce of *passatelli* (another traditional homemade pasta, made in Romagna, and prepared with Parmesan cheese, eggs, butter, flour and nutmeg) and fried nettle. Lastly, a fillet of pork stuffed with mushrooms and larded on a sauce of lentils, sausage and raisins, accompanied by a pumpkin, *raschera* (an Italian alps cheese) and mushrooms millefeuille.

Renowned Italian food journalist Aldo Fiordelli, in *d'Ex* magazine (August/September 2007), juxtaposed symbolically Bracali with a prestigious colleague: Alain Ducasse, the first chef to carry three Michelin stars in three different cities (Monte Carlo, Paris and New York). Over the years, Ducasse expanded his business, operating a number of restaurants all over the world: one of these was a prestigious Italian restaurant, the Trattoria Toscana in Castiglione della Pescaia, a luxurious resort on the Tirrenian sea, near Grosseto.

The comparison was intriguing for several reasons, not the least the geographic proximity of the two restaurants, located at about 40 miles' distance: but whereas Ghirlanda is a little-known name, Castiglione della Pescaia is a very popular tourist center. The two restaurants chose different ways of rereading the Tuscan gastronomic tradition: on the one hand, the noted Monégasque chef relied on authenticity, characterized by primary and immutable recipes, accomplished with the technique that can be expected from a world-famous name; on the other hand, the young and brilliant Maremma thoroughbred launched himself into exuberant reinventions. The immediacy to the limits of banality of Ducasse's baked cannelloni and grilled *migliacci* (a typical Tuscan dish made with fresh pig blood, raisins and pine nuts, similar to a pancake) was poles apart from Bracali's piglet *coppa* (a muscle of the pork right behind the back of the head, with a tasty combination of meat and fat, usually cured and served sliced thin as a cold cut) cooked in a crust of spices, whose balance had been studied for weeks in order to reach the desired result.

Fiordelli was one of the food journalists who followed more attentively Bracali's evolution over the years, and calibrated the critical judgment in step with the chef's human and professional growth; his article had the merit of setting very clearly a point of arrival in the history of the restaurant and in the mentality of the Bracali brothers.

> The dishes? Rich, opulent. Once the enthusiasm overflowed all over the menu, and each dish had a name so long that it occupied at least a couple of lines. Nowadays this is no longer the case: the menu is more synthetic, more clean, as in the work of those artists who grow and mature. An artist, yes, because Bracali is a 100% self-taught one.

The article continues: "

> When he serves you a dish, at first it is difficult to understand it. So many ingredients, different textures and temperatures, warm, cold.... The mind is disoriented, but the palate summarizes such complexity in a deep and exciting taste that doesn't need any culinary explanations.

Here, in short, is the miracle of Bracali's cuisine: the instinct, the *esprit de finesse* arrives where the *esprit géométrique* cannot: the palate, like the heart, has its own rules, which reason just cannot grasp.

The restyling marked the beginning of a new phase: a period of growth and popularity, with Bracali's participation in the gastronomic festival *Lo mejor de la gastronomia*, held in the Basque city of San Sebastián, and to the *Festa a Vico*, a three-day food event in the bay of Naples hosted by Gennarino Esposito, the two-Michelin-stars chef owner of the Torre del Saracino restaurant, located in Vico Equense. The Festa a Vico started in 2002, almost by chance: Esposito hosted the annual meeting of the JRE, which ended with a surprise after-party at Vico. The event was such a success that the guests suggested him that he repeat the party every year. The *Festa a Vico* became the occasion to celebrate food and friendship, giving room for young chefs to express their creativity, with hundreds of them cooking on the streets for thousands of food lovers from all over Italy: the food marathon climaxed with a charity dinner featuring Italy's top chefs.

These events, widely covered by the media and with an international resonation, underlined the newfound popularity of the food and wine world in the new millennium. This vast media exposure was characterized by a shift in balance: the web had now become central in the exploration and valorization of fine dining, while the guides were partially losing momentum. The early-to-mid 2000s saw the birth of a multitude of food blogs and websites: there, restaurant reviews were accompanied by photographs of the dishes, and the latter were often more interesting than the accompanying text. It was the beginning of a trend that would culminate in the phenomenon known as food porn.

On the other hand, this period was marked by various issues and painful events, separations and losses. Francesco reflects,

> I never had a very good relationship with my father, probably because we were too similar—in character, in appearance, in manners ... my father always wanted to have a son like Luca, more quiet and rational. Whereas I was the rebel, even though most of my rebellions ended immediately. I mean, I dyed my hair blond when I was thirty years old, and put an earring on at forty. These are things most people usually do in their teenage years, but I was not allowed to, because of my father's rigid nature. I mean, certain things were not allowed—full stop. Put an earring on? No way! Smoke a joint? To him, it was like shooting heroin. There was no middle ground. Whereas on the other hand I will be forever grateful to my father for the upbringing I was given. Even the manners at table, for example. At home, you were not allowed to show up at table without your shirt on, even in midsummer, because, he said, "Nobody ever died because of the heat," and you did not get up unless your parents had finished their meal. At dinner, you could not watch TV or read the newspaper, because it was the time for talking; sometimes you argued, but in the end it meant being all together, a whole family gathered around the table. There is a time for play and a time to sit at the table, he said. And nowadays, as an adult, when I see how parents find it hard to instill these concepts in their children, when I see children playing with their mobiles while eating distractedly, I understand he was right. I understand how important the idea of enjoying your meal as a convivial moment is, but not just for the act of eating, but because the communion it brings at so many levels. To confront and share. To look at each other and discuss. And to draw conclusions. In short, to allow each member of the family to share his or her daily experience. It is one of the deepest moments in a family's life.

Luciano Bracali had barely the chance to see the renovated restaurant. He was now detached from it—or rather, it was Francesco and Luca who asked him to step aside and let them carry on what he had started—but he kept visiting the place, riding his Vespa, and took on small errands, so as to maintain contact with the place where he had spent twenty years of his life. His marriage with Manuela had ended abruptly some time earlier, after the encounter with a younger woman, and the traumatic divorce had marked another turbulent step in the history of the family.

On that day of June 2004, a Monday, the restaurant was closed for the weekly day off. It was a bad day of torrential rain. Around 2 p.m., Luca called his father to see what he was doing. Luciano was on his way back from Grosseto, after some errands, and had stopped to pay a visit to a friend in the village of Roccastrada, about 45 minutes from the restaurant.

Luca too was about to drive to Grosseto and pick up some wine, and his father tried to make him changed his mind: "Your car tires are worn, and the weather is awful ... what is more, I have nothing to do. I'll pick it up first thing tomorrow morning, so you'll stay at the shop." He still called the restaurant "the shop," because to him it still was, even in its renewed form. However, Luca decided to go anyway, despite the weather. He had just returned to the restaurant, when the phone call arrived. It was his cousin, a doctor at the Grosseto hospital. She told him about the car accident, on the way down from Roccastrada. She did not venture into details, but Luca realized immediately, and ran home to warn his brother.

At the Grosseto morgue, the painful formality of recognition was up to Francesco. The following two days, he sat on the staircase leading to the mortuary chamber, his cap pulled down on his eyes, angrily smoking one cigarette after the other, without speaking to anyone. Without being able to squeeze a single tear.

> I'm not saying he was an angel, mind you. Were he still here with us, I would probably argue with him all the time as before. But he is the single person I miss the most. I miss the confrontations, the arguments, the relationship from man to man with an older person. Some time ago, walking down the streets of Massa Marittima, I came across a close friend of my father's. For a brief moment I saw him hesitant, as if he could not believe his eyes. Then he said: "Francesco, you really upset me. I saw the image of your dad in you." I am glad he did. It is as if I am still carrying my father inside me, and make him live again in my person. It is as if, after many years, I finally found my peace of mind.

But Francesco can also count his own physical scars, no less painful as the ones Anthony Bourdain described in his memoir *Kitchen Confidential*. In summer 2006 he severely fractured his right hand in a car accident: "I was dazzled by the sun at a roundabout, and while I pulled down the sun visor, the car in front of me braked abruptly. I hit my hand violently against the steering wheel, and I immediately realized that something bad had happened."

It was August 16, at the height of the tourist season, the highlight of the year for the restaurant: a broken hand meant forced inactivity, and Bracali could not afford it, not in that period, with the restaurant laboriously picking up a pace and the need to recover the costs of renovation. At the hospital he was so nervous that the nurses had a hard time sedating him for surgery. Eventually the surgeon agreed to apply an external fixator in the hand instead of plastering it. "'I am letting you out tomorrow,' the surgeon told me, 'but you have to promise that you won't move your hand for at least ten days.' The next day I was already working in the kitchen, trying to open and close my hand as best as I could, and the pain was almost unbearable. And when they removed the fixator, the hand was healed, but the knuckle of the ring finger was gone—it had slipped below."

In spite of all this, to Francesco it was a period of constant growth, both human and professional. Another important step was the trip to the United States, in New York, in 2007, and the one to Japan in September 2010: the immersion in such different cultures had miraculous effects in some ways, in addition to enriching his cultural and professional background.

In New York, Bracali participated in a gastronomic event organized by the famed San Domenico restaurant: for five evenings in a row he served a special tasting menu in collaboration with five wine producers, one different each evening. The experience was satisfying, even though Francesco and Luca realized very soon the diversity of raw materials compared with the ones they were used to dealing with in Maremma. "In New York, except for the meat which is outstanding—but usually it is cooked badly, and ends up burnt on the outside and therefore bitter at the taste—raw materials were absolutely not on a par with ours," Luca recalled.

> On the first of the five evenings, I was at the table with Nadia and other Italian guests, and when the first dish came to the table—red prawns with *lardo di Colonnata*—I immediately sensed that something was wrong. And the first bite confirmed my impression. It was impossible that my brother had forgotten how to cook overnight. And yet, that dish did not even remotely taste like the ones he used to prepare. I went to the kitchen to find out what was wrong, and it took us a glance to understand each other. "I know," he told me, "But what can I do? Instead of *lardo di colonnata* they provided me with bacon, saying that after all it was the same thing...."

Lardo di Colonnata is a type of cold cut made by curing strips of fatback with rosemary, herbs and spices. The pork meat is cured for months in basins made with marble from the Tuscan hamlet of Colonnata (near the town of Carrara, a site where marble is mined), and acquires an extremely delicate yet complex flavor and taste: sliced thinly and served with tomato, or paired with crustaceans, it is a true delight, so soft that it literally melts in the mouth. Substituting it with bacon is like, say, replacing white wine with whisky. The delicate balance of the dish was completely gone.

The thing Luca remembered with the greatest pleasure was going to dinner at Le Cirque and meeting one of the legends of Italian gastronomy, Sirio Maccioni. Born in Montecatini Terme, in Tuscany, in 1932, Maccioni left his hometown to escape poverty. He found a job in Paris, at the Florence: there, he became acquainted with the most famous stars—Serge Reggiani, Lino Ventura, Edith Piaf, Yves Montand. It was thanks to Montand—himself an Italian immigrant, born as Ivo Livi—that Maccioni got a job at the Place Athénée; after two years he became a waiter at the exclusive Maxim's. He then moved to Hamburg, and in the 1950s to America, where he became the maître at the Colony restaurant in New York. Finally, in March 1974, Maccioni opened his own restaurant, Le Cirque, at the Mayfair Hotel. In the 1980s Le Cirque became one of the Big Apple's most exclusive dining venues, with such regular guests as the then-President of the United States, Ronald Reagan. Maccioni's clientele included such names as Richard Nixon, Henry Kissinger, Frank Sinatra, Rudolph Giuliani, Aristotle Onassis.... To Luca, Sirio Maccioni was nothing short of a hero, and deservedly so.

He was really a character from another time. The true example of a complete restaurateur, one that is truly hard to find nowadays. A man who had left his hometown in Montecatini and created a gastronomic empire overseas. Nadia and I went to dinner, and he showed up at our table, and kissed the lady on the hand, impeccably. He had everything under control: he knew who I was, and immediately noticed that the sommelier had served me champagne in a flute unfit for the wine. Professional, impeccable, and a magnificent host.

Nevertheless, Luca's experience at Le Cirque was not all roses.

It's a legendary place, full of stars, divas, models ... but the kitchen just did not measure up to the expectations. It was one of my worst experiences in a gourmet restaurant. With the aggravation of the double shifts: service works like a clock, but at ten o'clock the waiter shows up and asks you to kindly leave the table, for there are other guests to accommodate. Something like this would be unthinkable in a fine dining Italian restaurant, where the table is yours all evening and you can stay as long as you will. It is a matter of hospitality. Anyway, there was a recent review by Pete Wells in the *New York Times* which summarized my thoughts: "The kitchen gave the impression that it had stopped reaching for excellence and possibly no longer remembered what that might mean." And personally, the day I realize that my brother and I have stopped reaching for excellence, that would be the day when I'll call myself out of the game.

Francesco Bracali's journey to Japan was organized by Yukio Ishizaki, the executive chef in two important restaurants of the Suzuya group, with the cinephile name *La vita è bella*. Four days at the Nasu-Kogen in the district of Nasu, in the Tochigi Prefecture, north of Tokyo, and four more days at the Izu-Kogen on the hills of Shizuoka, about 120 miles south of the Capital. Two luxury restaurants: the first is located in a resort surrounded by a luxurious vegetation, and built like an old English castle, the second on top of a green and panoramic hill in front of the Philippine Sea, in a building which recalls a big European manor house of the Middle Ages. Bracali prepared different tasting menus for each occasion, and took advantage of the trip to learn something more about the habits and customs of Japanese gastronomy.

> One evening we went to eat at a tiny restaurant, which looked like a set from an Ozu film. To enter, you had to lower your head, and behind the counter there was a septuagenarian chef, stern-looking and deeply deferential. Dinner was served by an elderly lady in a colored, beautiful silk kimono, and we ate on low tables, crouched on the cushions. We ate sashimi served on peach flowers, and I was struck by the perfection and the suaveness of the presentation, opulent yet at the same time extremely fine. There it was: linearity, cleanliness, intended as the arrangement and harmony of the elements on the plate, aesthetic exquisiteness. All factors which I think I have fully grasped thanks to my journey in Japan.

This period of professional growth culminated with the second Michelin star, awarded to the Bracali restaurant in November 2010. A long-awaited goal, but which came at a rather unexpected time. "It was the most difficult moment, economically and professionally, since we had opened, and there had been lots of hard times," Francesco recalled. "Nadia and I had split the previous year, and there were only three people working in the kitchen: me, my sous chef Marco Violini (who then opened a restaurant on his own, the Osteria del Vento in Montecarlo, near Lucca) and a young lad who was staging at the restaurant, Gianluca Buccianti."

Like any other year, the Michelin inspector made his appearance during the spring. It is customary for Michelin inspectors to dine anonymously (although, as Luca maintains, a good restaurateur immediately recognizes one...) and introduce themselves only after dinner. Apparently, the inspector was very satisfied with the meal, even though as usual he did not say too much. But the real surprise came in July, when the then-director of the Italian Michelin Guide himself, Fausto Arrighi, booked a table at the restaurant. When the Number One guy showed up, it became obvious that something was cooking. Francesco and Luca awaited that day with some nervousness.

Unfortunately, though, the evening did not seem to bode well. Or, at least, that was Luca's sensation. Arrighi had a strong headache, and ate only a couple of dishes, but he praised the bread and the sorbet cart. He left without saying a word. Luca and Francesco did not hear from him until late autumn. By then, Francesco had lost all hopes. "On Tuesday, November 24, in Milan, there would be the presentation of the 2011 Michelin Guide. The previous Thursday I was in Milan for a dinner, and we returned to Massa Marittima on Friday. The phone rang, and Gianluca answered. 'Someone wants to speak to you, Francesco,' he said, 'a Mr. Arrighi.'"

Those who know the man won't be surprised of Arrighi's extreme, almost enigmatic discretion. During his years as director, the Michelin Guide was top secret until the day it came out: no indiscretions (and indeed, the circulating rumors often proved wrong) among journalists or even the same chefs. And that day, on the phone, Arrighi was cryptic to say the least. "'Francesco, will you come to Milan for the presentation, next Tuesday?' I didn't know what to think. 'Director, if I am invited, with pleasure!' And since unlike other guides, Michelin invites a chef only if something is cooking, I ventured to ask: 'Director, but is there any news?' And he replied: 'Every year there's some news!' That was all I managed to know from him."

The next Tuesday, hopeful but still in complete uncertainty, Francesco arrived in Milan.

I did not know anything until I checked in at the Principe di Savoia Hotel. By the way, upon walking past the door in the hall I found myself in front of a bunch of screaming girls. It was a moment of disorientation: to have become a star overnight without knowing it was a little too much! (laughs) And then I realized I was rubbing shoulders with Robbie Williams, who was in Milan for a show!

Arrighi was standing in the conference room by a huge table with all the jackets prepared for the starred chefs, which we would put on for the press conference. "Go look for your jacket," he said. "Director, now you can tell me..." Nothing. "Pick up your jacket." I took it, and saw the two stars embroidered on the chest.

That jacket would remain his own for just a few hours—the luck of the Bracalis. After the press conference, on the way to the station, a journalist of the *Gambero Rosso* magazine called Francesco for an interview. Since he was in a crowded and noisy bar, he went out for a few moments to speak freely and avoid the confusion, leaving inside the bag with the guide and the jacket. When he came back inside, the bag was gone. However, the two stars would stay and shine on his restaurant, and that was what really mattered.

Challenge to Change

The second Michelin star was an award worth a thousand disappointments, a light which illuminated the darkest days. An international recognition which, if on one hand gratified Bracali and made him proud, on the other put him in a position of even more responsibility, and vulnerability. The type of challenge that stimulates his ego even more.

The relationship with the other major guides was more problematic. On the one hand, *L'Espresso* never stopped believing in Bracali, and awarded him high votes. In the July 2014 issue, the director Enzo Vizzari penned an article, "Maremma creativa," where he magnified the "Tuscan talent," and highly praised two dishes in particular, the pigeon and the nettle gnocchi (more on which later). With the 2017 edition, the guide substituted the votes from 1 to 20 with a scale expressed in chef hats, from 1 to 5. Bracali was awarded three hats and voted the best restaurant in Tuscany. On the other hand, the *Gambero Rosso* never fully appreciated Bracali's talent, and the restaurant did not achieve the three forks.

But more awards, no less special, were to come. From 2012 to 2015 Bracali was also executive chef at the restaurant Il Poggio Rosso in Borgo San Felice, a prestigious five-star luxury hotel of the Relais & Chateaux circuit, in Castelnuovo Berardenga, near Siena: an ancient medieval hamlet in the Chianti countryside, surrounded by vines and olive trees, frequented by an international clientele, and not far from the major Tuscan tourist sites (Siena, San Gimignano, Volterra, Montalcino...). Its director, Achille Di Carlo, wanted to give the place a world class restaurant, by hiring a renowned chef, similarly to what other luxury hotels in Tuscany had done before. Alain Ducasse's Trattoria Toscana had been one of the first examples, and even the English celebrity chef Gordon Ramsay had been hired as a consultant in the nearby Castel Monastero hotel.

Such moves were a further sign of the growing appeal of Tuscany all over the world, but also a hint of the mass globalization of the restaurant business, with the choice of famous names aimed at pleasing a varied international clientele and gaining publicity without much attention to the peculiarities and the gastronomic identity of the place. Whereas Ducasse's rendition of Tuscan dishes was so bare-bones that it bore almost no trace whatsoever of the chef's own personality, Ramsay's rendition of the terroir was a lazy by-the-numbers "modernization" of tradition, resulting in dishes that retained very little of the original spirit but were not creative enough to spark interest in the average food enthusiasts.

The experience offered Francesco the chance of an international spotlight, but came at the cost of an unprecedented work commitment. Unlike Ducasse and Ramsay, who barely ever set foot in their Tuscan branch after the first, and well-publicized, photo shoots, Bracali took the commitment very seriously, and for the best part of three years he divided himself between his own restaurant in Ghirlanda and Borgo San Felice.

It was not an easy task. One thing is to open a new dining venue, another is to enter into an existing reality and bring it to a new light. Until then, in the common perception, Il Poggio Rosso was considered a good hotel restaurant, but nothing to write home about, and its menu did not offer the extra something which the beautiful environment and luxurious context would demand. It was up to Bracali to add that extra something.

To him, this was not a mere technical consultancy, limited to lending his own name to the project. Francesco personally redesigned all the menus, from the room service to the breakfast, from the brunch to the pool bar. His determination to keep everything under control led him to sacrifice his days off and stay two days a week at Borgo Felice, so as to keep direct contact with the resident head chef, whom he personally chose and instructed.

It was yet another challenge. "Having grown both professionally and humanly in a restricted ambience—after all, cooking at the restaurant to me is and has always been like cooking at home, because that *is* my home—at the beginning I had to coordinate a crew of many more individuals, in a different ambience and with different demands—a high profile cuisine for a much greater number of guests, ensuring consistent quality even in large numbers." In addition to the different numbers to handle (a dining room with 150 seats instead of the 25 in Ghirlanda), Bracali had to rethink his style radically. He could not simply offer a duplicate of the same dishes from his own restaurant, whose uniqueness had to be preserved, and he also had to consider the needs of a different type of clientele—not only those ones who would usually drive hundreds of miles to sit at his table, but also those who, not being fine dining lovers, would not be impressed by his style, but on the contrary could even be disappointed by the lack of "typical" regional dishes.

The only choice was compromise: Bracali decided to stick to his style and offer some of his signature dishes, such as the pigeon with foie gras, carrot and chocolate sauce, but he also offered his own interpretation of the traditional Chianti cuisine, by sticking to quality raw materials of the territory, which on average are richer than those to be found in Maremma. In doing this, he kept faithful to the territorial tradition and its gastronomic roots, which he reinvented and enriched according to his own vision, without distorting them.

The result was promising, and Bracali's felicitous collaboration with the talented Gianluca Gorini (who had previously worked with the brilliant, idiosyncratic Paolo Lopriore, one of Italy's most experimental, countercurrent chefs) seemed to open the way for the first Michelin star. However, Gorini left after only one year, to start a new adventure on his own at Le Giare, in the village of Montenovo di Montiano, in the region of Romagna, where he offered a drastically more experimental kitchen, and 2013 was a very troubled year. Only in July Bracali finally managed to find a good substitute, Alessandra Zacchei, flanked by her pastry chef husband Nazzareno Dodi. Il Poggio Rosso recovered its course, and in 2014 a second restaurant opened in the hotel, focused on a more traditional Tuscan cooking style, with such specialties as the Maremma tortelli, a mouth-watering dish which Aldo Fiordelli described as follows: "At least a hand's palm wide, with a typically Tuscan-thin pastry stuffed with ricotta and spinach, with a huge spoonful of gravy in the middle and grated Parmesan cheese dolloped on top of it in full view, with nonchalance." A basic simplicity which synthesizes the correct approach to tradition, too often destroyed by carelessness and improvisation.

The Michelin star never came, though, and in 2015 the collaboration ended. Nevertheless, the experience in Borgo San Felice was felicitous. Francesco was called to organize pharaonic Russian weddings, and in October 2013 he and his team prepared a dinner for Albert II, Prince of Monaco, during a charity event for the prince's foundation. It was an important goal for a chef who had started literally from nothing, but whose cuisine had always been princely in concept and taste.

The following years were filled with awards and participations to special events which strengthened Bracali's reputation as one of the country's best chefs and also shaped his character. The shy young man seen in those old pictures in *La Cucina Italiana* had been replaced by a mature and self-confident professional, fully in charge of his own feelings.

In March 2017, Francesco was a special guest at the prestigious fes-

Francesco Bracali in Cortona, March 2017, for the food and wine event "Chianina & Syrah" (courtesy Terretrusche Events; photograph by Valerio Paterni).

tival "Chianina & Syrah: Dalle Stalle alle Stelle" (Chianina & Syrah: from the Stables to the Stars). The three-day cultural and gastronomic event aimed at valorizing two enogastronomic staples of the Tuscan province of Arezzo and specifically the Valdichiana area around the Etruscan town of Cortona, where it took place: the beef from the *Chianina* breed of cattle, which is considered one of the finest in the world, and Syrah red wine.

The event included roundtable conferences, cooking shows, wine tastings, documentary screenings and a gala dinner with the participation of several noted Michelin-starred chefs, including Francesco's old mentor Gaetano Trovato, Paolo Gramaglia (of the one-starred restaurant President in Pompeii), Silvia Baracchi (chef and owner of the one-starred restaurant and relais Il Falconiere in Cortona), and Bracali. Each chef presented a dish with his or her interpretation of the Chianina, paired with some of the area's finest wines.

Francesco's dish was his version of beef tartare. The following day he described the creation of this extraordinary dish in detail on a local cooking show. The episode received acclaim for Bracali's obvious love and deep

Top: Fausto Arrighi (ex-director of the Italian Michelin guide) and Francesco Bracali, enjoy each other's company at "Chianina & Syrah" in Cortona, in 2017. *Bottom:* Gaetano Trovato (two-Michelin-stars chef and owner of Arnolfo, in Colle Val d'Elsa) and Francesco Bracali, collaborate (courtesy Terretrusche Events; photograph by Valerio Paterni).

From left to right: Fausto Arrighi, Gaetano Trovato and Francesco Bracali, together for "Chianina & Syrah," 2017 (courtesy Terretrusche Events; photograph by Valerio Paterni).

knowledge of the region's gastronomic specialties and his sincere devotion to highlighting the ingredients' qualities and peculiarities, while at the same time remaining true to his own, unmistakable philosophy of food.

For Luca serenity came after a long labor. It was accompanied by a clarity of judgment that not everyone is given to achieve after such serious and painful experiences as the long rehabilitation. Others, unlike him, have surrendered, or at least they have never been able to reach an inner compromise. That was the case with Yari, the wood worker who built the cheese trolley: a severe disability made his right arm completely numb, and after a few years he had to abandon his job. Luca tried in vain to help him: "Yari never accepted his situation, and one day I really got angry at him," he recalls,

I wanted to make him understand that having a disability is something you have to accept in your heart. But not because there is someone beside you who accepts you for what you are—someday, that someone might not be with you anymore, and then you'd have to start all over again. It's not easy, that's obvious. There are people who see their own disability as a challenge against everyone and everything, and get really emotional about it. Sure, moving from the wheelchair to the crutches is a challenge, and I know very well what it means. But it must be a challenge in a positive sense, not something that's eating you inside day after day, and wears you down, making you die little by little inside.

Accepting yourself is fundamental, both in the relationship with your partner and at work. Here, at the restaurant, when I am always wearing suit and tie, my clothes partially conceal my situation. But at home, when I take off my shoes, I walk badly, and on my legs and arms there are still all the scars left by the accident and the many surgeries, and all this is something you will have to share with someone else in your intimacy, if you have a relationship with someone.

This doesn't mean I don't think about my disability at all. But I metabolized it. Either the other person accepts it or not. But what is truly important, in my opinion, is that you have to be able to accept your own impairments in the first place, if they allow you to live a more or less normal life. You have to give things their proper importance, and never be conditioned by other people's eyes looking at you. It's a form of self-protection—I wouldn't say egoistic, but necessary.

"Same thing at the restaurant," Luca recalls. After the accident, he has never been able to bend his elbow correctly, and this is evident in the way he writes or he pours wine in the glass.

One evening I took an order, and seeing me write on my notebook in a weird way, a lady asked me: "Why are you writing like that?" "Why?," I would have liked to answer, "Because I just like it that way...." Same with people watching me as I walk, staring at my orthopedic shoe. But you have to get to live with all that, without ruining your life, or ruining it to the people who live beside you, and who care about you. Without ever victimizing yourself.

This, of course, is even more important in everyday life.

The Luca Bracali who goes on the beach on Sunday in the summer is completely different from the one who serves wine and food in the dining room. Because on the beach I limp, I often lose my balance, and I need someone to lean on ... but I go to the beach nonetheless. At first it was difficult, and for three or four years I never even wanted to hear about it. Then, one day, someone—a friend, my fiancée, my brother, I don't remember—told me: "You know what? I've had enough of that. Let's go to the beach!" The first day it was tough, I could feet people's eyes on me all the time. Then I thought: Hey, come on, the beach belongs to everybody, I have my own towel and I'm not bothering anyone. Let's relax and enjoy the sun. And if the others are good with that, fine; or else, that's none of my business.

Three

Classicity and Experimentation

Instinct and Creation

There is a photograph of Francesco Bracali, sitting on an armchair in the lounge room of his restaurant, holding what at a casual glance would seem a recipe volume. Only at a closer look one realizes that in fact that's not a book but a vinyl record: the first self-titled album by The Velvet Underground, with Andy Warhol's legendary banana on the cover. An unexpected but apt image, because if it is true that there were chefs who created dishes inspired by songs, musicians, artist and works of art, in the case of Francesco Bracali the relationship with artistic expression is tighter and more complex.

Like one of his teenage idols, Michael Jackson, Bracali moved within the territories of *haute cuisine* with an impressive tenacity and energy. He never copied anyone, but he always sought in himself the inspiration to create new dishes, instead of songs or dance steps. And he managed to create a style—totally, unmistakably his own. A dish by Francesco Bracali doesn't look like anything but a dish by Francesco Bracali, and one can recognize it immediately as such: not at first bite, not at first sight, but even just by reading its composition and glimpsing the concept behind it.

Bracali's idea of cuisine is one that speaks to the heart and is driven by instinct, but which brings with itself a most rigorous creative process. Each dish takes shape on paper, in the form of a drawing that anticipates and fixates its final form, in the manner painters and sculptors set on

Bracali and the Revolution in Tuscan Cuisine

One of Bracali's latest creations: veal tongue with Parmesan emulsion, small cubes of smoked broth, wheat grain bread.

paper the basic ideas of a new project. "Every time I create a dish in my head, it is very unlikely that I change my mind during its preparation," the chef explained in a 2005 interview. "Instinct brings me to a constant desire to try out new combinations, following the natural season cycle. Therefore, it is equally unlikely that I repeat the same dish over time, even though it was particularly appreciated by my guests." It is a brave move, on the part of a chef who has created dozens and dozens of dishes, all very elaborate and most of them memorable, to leave behind the certainty of a successful creation and embark on a new challenge. But everything flows, and one must look to the future.

Bracali elaborated on his peculiar style as follows:

I always tried to be a sponge, in some situations, whereas in others I tried to be impermeable. I mean, during my path I tried to absorb whatever notions I could from my colleagues, the suppliers, and the people I worked with—butchers, farmers, fishermen ... in order to gain the knowledge and technique necessary to devise my own vision. On the other hand, I rejected the idea of "borrowing from" or "being inspired by" the current fad in the gastronomic world, and went along my own path, with many missteps indeed. But I rarely, if ever, limited myself to offering what I could find in the market in basic preparations. Neither did I stick to what the common tendencies demanded.

Luca appreciates his brother's approach to food:

Francesco has always kept a low profile, compared to some chefs who have become TV stars. Low profile, but high performances. Not humility, mind you: he doesn't need that. He does not allow himself to be swayed by the mood of the moment, the current fad, and so on. That's his strength, his biggest merit, and something which makes him unlike the vast majority of his colleagues. Even the most prestigious names, every now and then, pay a price to the fashion of the day, so as to show that they are still "into the game," so to speak. Whereas Francesco just doesn't need to. If he puts, say, a *lièvre à la royale* in the menu, it is not because it has become fashionable again, but because he believes he has found his own interpretation of the dish.

"The same happens with the interior decoration, the design, etcetera," Francesco points out. "To me, if I like something and Luca likes it too, then my whole world likes it, and that's enough. Full stop."

This is particularly remarkable, at a moment when Italian *haute cuisine* seems to be on the verge of a nervous breakdown: on the one hand, many young chefs come to the limelight, and are often saluted as the next big thing by the press and the media, whereas on the other there is a diffused feeling of a lack of evolution, and creative stagnation. Experimentation is often reduced to technical showiness, a mannerist game which satisfies the eye but brings very little to a dish in terms of conception and innovation. A large part of the responsibility relies on the way the food and wine world functions.

Since the early 2000s, communication has been taken over by food blogs and websites, which have granted a much wider stage to the gastronomy world and created an army of food enthusiasts. Still, there are only few truly prepared food journalists in Italy, a small community which includes such deans as Enzo Vizzari and Luigi Cremona, who maintain a rigorous approach to their job. Their knowledge of the matter is so deep and varied that they can understand every nuance of a dish with only a few bites: the name of Cremona's own blog, *Porzioni Cremona* (Cremona portions) is a joke on the journalist's acknowledged habit of tasting just tiny bits of food during his visits to restaurants. Not by chance, these food experts have immediately understood the personality and uniqueness of Bracali's cuisine since his very first steps, and helped him to become more mature.

Assembling a dish in the kitchen is a precision work.

Other bloggers are simply food enthusiasts who started dining around, took pictures and put their impressions in their blogs. Some are reliable, others do not really have any deep knowledge about gastronomy. To put it bluntly, to be an alcoholic does not make one a wine specialist— does it? Most of these "reviews" consists merely of "food porn" pictures—

mostly very well taken—accompanied by a few banal lines which summarily describe the dishes (or barely repeat the name as indicated on the menus), but rarely venture into any real critical analysis.

The relationship between bloggers and food journalists on one side and restaurateurs on the other is a complex and delicate one. And, unlike with, say, film critics and movie directors, it is personal. Normally, a film critic goes to the theater or to a festival, watches a movie and writes down a review in the newspaper (or in his blog...) without ever meeting the filmmaker—unless he attends a press conference where, however, there is hardly a direct exchange of ideas, but basically a question/answer routine. A food critic shows up at the restaurant, eats the food and drinks the wine, and often has a chat with the chef. A different kind of relationship is established. And, more often than not, a chef will do his best to make the other comfortable, either offering a bottle of champagne, sending extra tasting bits from the kitchen, or even offering the whole meal. In a way, it is a form of psychological subjection.

In addition to that, some food writers will show up at a restaurant and not pay for the dinner: rather, there will be a mutual exchange of favors, and the next day a favorable or enthusiastic review will appear, complete with glamorous pics of the various delicacies tasted during the dinner. An unspoken habit, but quite common in the gastronomy world, which nevertheless puts a chef in a somehow difficult position. Some critics are adamant about the necessity of staying anonymous, like the Michelin Guide inspectors, who will reveal themselves only afterwards, and always pay for their meal. This has led to ferocious controversy in the new media.

Then there is the competition for visibility. Many chefs enroll top-notch photographers (or rather, they are talked into enrolling them by the photographers themselves, since photographing food has become a real business) to create a cool portfolio. More and more, *haute cuisine* is becoming a visual art rather than one that deals with the palate: since it is very difficult to explain how a dish tastes, it is much easier to show how it *looks*.

Tradition and Innovation

Several years ago, Francesco Bracali and Valeria Piccini were in Milan, attending an edition of *Identità Golose* (Gourmet Identities), the first

Bracali and the Revolution in Tuscan Cuisine

gastronomic congress dedicated to signature cuisine and pastry making created in 2004 by food journalist Paolo Marchi. They attended a lecture by Heston Blumenthal, the chef of Michelin three-star British restaurant The Fat Duck, famous for his idiosyncratic, thought-provoking creations. Blumenthal explained to his audience that for years he had been interested in the external sensory triggers that shape a dining experience, from the multi-sensory process of flavor perception to the way context effects taste. Blumenthal cited experiments that test the effects of sounds, colors and smells on the perception of flavor and texture, and introduced one of his signature dishes, Sound of the Sea. It recalled an aquarium, where the seafood was presented on a glass-topped wooden box containing sand and seashells, and it consisted of what looked like sand but was in fact a mixture of tapioca, fried breadcrumbs, crushed fried baby eels, cod liver oil and langoustine oil topped with abalone, razor clams, shrimps and oysters and three kinds of edible seaweed. The final touch, and the culmination of Blumenthal's experiments exploring the relationship between sound and the experience of eating, was an iPod so that diners could listen to the sound of the sea while they ate the dish.

The audience roared with applause, but Bracali was less favorably impressed.

> I'm not discussing the technique here: he is obviously a great chef. What I sense is a different problem: it is not right—or rather, it is not educational—to present dishes like this one to an eighteen-year-old kid who has just finished school and wants to become a chef. Because that very kid, once he shows up in my restaurant to learn the job, will immediately want to learn those type of dishes. He will want to learn about liquid nitrogen, foams, show-stopping presentations. And he will forget that, first and foremost, one must learn the basics.

After Blumenthal had finished his lecture, it was the turn of another prestigious chef: Lidia Alciati, the wife of Guido Alciati. The couple had opened their restaurant Guido in Costigliole d'Asti, Piedmont, in 1960. It was one of the very first gourmet restaurants in Italy, offering a traditional cuisine with class: recipes based on territory and seasonal raw materials, a nice and elegant dining room, prestigious wines. The Alciatis' signature recipe were the *Agnolotti del plin*, a traditional stuffed pasta typical of the Piedmont region, handmade and with a filling consisting primarily of roasted meat. The agnolotti are formed by pinching the dough in-between the individual agnolotto, "*plin*" being the Piemontese word for "pinch." In her lecture, Lidia explained the correct technique for pinching the pasta.

Francesco describes a response far less enthusiastic than Blumenthal's special effects-ridden, hi-tech creations received.

> The room literally emptied. Many did not even know who Lidia was—they did not even know about Guido, a pillar of Italian gastronomy. It was a very serious gap: I mean, it was like studying history and ignoring who Napoleon Bonaparte was. Guido Alciati has been a pioneer of Italian cuisine, 50 years in the business, internationally known from generations! When Lidia went down the stage, limping, with the help of crutches—she was very ill, and would pass away in August 2010—there were just three of us, who had stayed to say hello and pay our respects to her—me, Valeria and another chef. We chatted for a while, and Lidia began to tell us her story: the beginnings, the difficulties, the empty restaurant. During those first, harsh few months, she would burst out crying in the kitchen because of all the debts they had, but her husband insisted on not accepting any guest without a reservation. It was as if my own past resurfaced before my eyes: the story was the same, and on our part we had undergone the very same sacrifices as Lidia and Guido, to try and create the type of restaurant we had in our mind. It was an extremely moving moment. And I think nowadays the younger generations should learn about these things, and listen carefully to these stories. Instead, all they want is to become TV celebrities. Their idea of being a chef is more similar to a rock star than to somebody who cooks food for other people.

His reaction reveals much about his own position in the Italian gastronomic world, today. Once a boy wonder, a self-taught kid who had landed like an alien among the great starred chefs with his irreverent, seemingly chaotic creations, nowadays Francesco Bracali almost looks like a *laudator temporis acti*, one who praises past time only, compared with the ranks of young chefs armed with siphon and liquid nitrogen and launched to the conquest of TV broadcasts. Quite simply, Bracali is now a classic himself, far from compromises and current fashions, and as such he cannot help but considering himself the keeper of a tradition which he feels he must preserve and defend.

> Nowadays we live on income of certain things. Those people, like Marchesi or Alciati, were those who have created a certain audience, and had restaurants follow certain rules in order to elevate themselves. Nowadays you are accustomed to book a table even when you go out for a pizza, but once it was not like that. And I feel it is important for young aspiring chefs to know the history of Italian gastronomy, and the path that led it to excellence...

Understandably, Bracali's deepest relationships with his colleagues are with those who shared his journey, and with whom he has an immediate understanding, despite the inevitable highs and lows over the years. One such is Moreno Cedroni. Bracali came across him after several years

Francesco and Luca Bracali today.

in Milan, during an edition of *Identità Golose*, where they had to do a cooking show at the Longino & Cardinal stand. Founded in the 1990s, Longino & Cardenal is a company specialized in providing top-quality foods and primary ingredients to high-end Italian restaurants. Bracali describes the set up,

Three—Classicity and Experimentation

There were four of us: me, Moreno, pastry chef Ernst Knam and Sergio Mei, the chef from Milan's Four Seasons hotel, another cornerstone of Italian fine dining from the years of Marchesi and Paracucchi. Longino had made available for us several products: Bresse chicken, wild boar, and so on. I was a bit on the sidelines, since I am not particularly at ease during these events. Then Moreno came to me, with his boyish smile, and said: "Francesco, we have a wild boar here, and you're from Maremma, so it's up to you to prepare it...." We hadn't heard from each other in years, but in that moment something clicked, without the need for many words. We were a team, and as such we had that bond that forms when, say, two musicians are jamming together on a jazz standard. Thinking in tune, so to speak, and understanding each other in the blink of an eye, because this is what we do and what we know. So we started to work together on this wild boar, with what we had at our disposal. Moreno offered to prepare the sauce: "What if we pair the boar with a soft fruits sauce?" Problem was, we didn't have any berries. Moreno winked at me: "Wait, I got it!" And without a word he went to the fridge ... and fetched the raspberries that Ernst Knam should have used for a cake, like a boy stealing the marmalade from his mother's pantry.... When we presented the boar, I could see a puzzled look on Knam's face. Then he realized—he ran to the fridge, looked inside and found out that his berries were missing! I'll never forget the expression he had when he turned round to us—Moreno and I just could not stop laughing. At first he was really pissed off, and rightly so, but in the end he had a big laugh too, and the evening was a success.

Other colleagues who Bracali deeply respects are Massimiliano Alajmo, the former child prodigy of Le Calandre, "because of the clarity and simplicity with which he manifests his formidable authority," Pino Cuttaia (the chef owner of the Michelin-two-stars restaurant La Madia, in Licata, Sicily), and Gennaro Esposito. All of them propose a type of cuisine that eschews fireworks, fashion and homologation, without sacrificing their strong, unmistakable personality. "In my opinion, currently there is too much standardization in restaurants, both in techniques and recipes. If a big name comes up with his own interpretation of the lièvre à la royale, then be sure that soon there will be other ten, fifteen, twenty others who will introduce it in their menus within the blink of an eye. That's the way it works nowadays, and it's not good for creativity."

Francesco Bracali's interpretation of Tuscan cuisine has a fundamental creative and experimental drive, but nowadays it can be defined as "classical," in the best and noblest sense of the term. Despite the elaborate concepts behind many of his dishes, the results are classical because of the way they aim at the absolute balance of taste, while dealing with ingredients that are apparently incompatible, and because of the chef's tendency to add rather than to remove. To Bracali, it has been written, the ideal way to connect two dots is not a straight line, but a doodle.

Francesco at work in the kitchen.

Sense and Sensibility

Bracali does not love minimalism. It does not suit his conception. Each dish must be a challenge, and the ultimate goal is the squaring of the circle. This means he is not afraid of bundling too many concepts, nor does he bend to compromises, and he is willing to do anything to reach the result he has in mind—that is, as he calls it, his "mental palate."

The result of a professional and interior journey, it took years to achieve it, an endless series of trials and errors, with no short cuts.

There was no one by my side telling me that one ingredient would suit better with another one, and so on. I tried and discovered everything on my own. I would say that these thirty years were a continuous approximation and improvement that finally brought me to this. I can create a dish in my head, I mean I can envision the whole process from start to finish, and I know perfectly well how the result will be, how will it taste, and what I have to do in order to achieve it. I don't have any prejudice on the ingredients, nor on any technical procedure to apply. I only think about the final result, the amalgamation of individual flavors and textures, according to my own taste.

84

Very often, such procedure is not accomplished by following the cooking books by numbers: Francesco will go along his own path, which sometimes will be tortuous and never followed before, but it will lead him exactly where he wants.

I need the procedure to be mine, and mine only. The technique and the knowledge of raw materials are essential, but they are instrumental to allow me to reach the goal I have in mind, not an end in themselves. The beauty of a dish is also given by the beauty of the whole creating process itself. This also brought me to the discovery of certain products and ingredients, as well as of the hidden correspondences between them. In a way, it is like having a library all for yourself, and starting reading all those books, one by one. Book after book, the more you read, the more you'll discover wonderful, unexpected things, and points of contact, and new concepts and ideas will come to your mind. You'll expand your knowledge and sensibility, and look at the world with new eyes. What I mean is, it's not a cold, theoretic approach to cooking, but a more emphatic, genuine, humane one.

Assembling a dish.

Here is how, with his creations, Bracali tries to grasp points of contact or unexpected complementarities between raw materials, and in the meantime he reflects on the taste of a certain food, not in itself but in relation to a thousand others. The way he moves within this universe of tastes, textures, aromas, colors recalls a painter's palette, from which to take fresh inspiration to create something new, like the Macchiaioli painters who broke with the antiquated conventions taught by the Italian academies of art, and did much of their painting outdoors, in order to capture light, shade, and color. In

85

doing so, they led the way to Italian modern painting. Back then, they were innovators; nowadays, they are classics.

One name that has often compared to Francesco Bracali's style—more because of elective affinities rather than for concrete similarities—is that of Gianfranco Vissani. Born in Umbria in 1951, in the 1980s Vissani had established himself as some sort of mad genius of Italian gastronomy, thanks to his knowledge and practice of the international cuisine combined with the variety of flavors, freshness and fantasy of the local cuisine. Vissani became one of the first celebrity chefs in Italy, often appearing on television, having his own personal column in newspapers, and publishing several recipe books.

Vissani's no-holds barred approach to ingredient pairings and infallible "mental palate" are very similar to Bracali's, as is his disdain for fashion, often expressed in strong tirades in the press. Enzo Vizzari once labeled Bracali "the Tuscan Vissani," and Francesco still recalls the incredibly strong emotions he felt during his first dinner at Vissani's two-starred restaurant in Civitella del Lago, on the Lake Corbara, many years ago. As Aldo Fiordelli wrote, "Bracali's brilliance is exciting, because of the sheer succession of flavors. The same as at Vissani's, but with fewer spotlights on the chef, and more on the dishes themselves."

Bracali resembles Vissani also in his ongoing rush toward the future, and in the refusal to settle into a routine made of repetition, even at the cost of sacrificing exceptional dishes, which in his view are no longer representative of his style. An example is the Leghorn chicken salad with cooked must, foie gras and Parmesan ice cream, one of the most beloved items on the menu, which nevertheless was put aside in favor of other interpretations of poultry dishes.

Beyond the superficial comparison between the two chefs, however, the taste for challenge, as well as the search for inspiration in the colors and flavors of the season, and in nature's continuous renewal, reveal Bracali's stubbornness and willpower. He needs to continually relaunch the game, and he is well aware of being able to do so while remaining true to himself, even in diversity. As he explains it, "My cuisine must "talk" about me, and send message in a language that is true to itself, but in a continuous evolution. This means to hone and grow an already defined style."

As Luca loves to say: "When you taste a dish by Bracali, you understand it at the very last bite." That is, its concept and remarkable complexity are fully displayed only at the end, unlike many dishes which reveal themselves immediately, at first bite, and then lose their interest, as they lack depth, nuances, complexity. The same, to Luca, can be said about a good wine.

Luigi Veronelli used to say that you never judge a good wine with the first sip, but starting with the second. You know, there are wines that immediately strike you as soon as you put them under your nose and smell. It's like noticing an attractive, elegantly-dressed woman passing you by, walking in a sexy way on high heels. You look at her, and think, 'Wow, she is gorgeous!' But let's suppose you get to meet that woman and ask her for a date, and she agrees. You go out, chat, speak of this and that, and realize that she is not the most intelligent type. You know what I mean? Anyway, let's go further. Suppose you and this attractive woman have a one-night stand, like consenting adults do. Next morning you wake up, and watch your partner. Without all her make-up, her stylish dresses, and so on, she doesn't look so attractive the morning after. Her green eyes were the result of colored contact lenses; her skin is pockmarked; her breath is bad. Here, this is like some wines are—they smell and taste great at first, but it's just the first impression. Once you get to know them better, they are not quite so good as you first thought. Sometimes, they are a travesty. And frankly, these are not the types of wine—and women—I care about. On the other hand, let's suppose you meet a pretty girl. Pretty, not gorgeous, and dressed in a rather unassuming way. And yet you notice that she has beautiful, intense eyes, fine complexion, perfect bone structure. But she does not feel the need to show her beauty off. So you take her out on a date, and discover she is smart, cultured, has a great sense of humor, and all that. But if you had judged her from the first glimpse, you'd never have noticed all that. Same with some wines, which you appreciate more and more after each taste—I would say that you appreciate them fully when you finish the bottle. And these are the wines that I like and I try to suggest to my guests, for a full experience in tune with Francesco's kitchen.

Luca's approach to wine tasting is equally independent and idiosyncratic, often poles apart from the usual sommelier routine.

I am not having a lecture on wine, when I serve it at the table. The guests could not care less about the technical details. I fully sympathize with those who think sommeliers are full of shit when they start with their mumbo jumbo ritual, that empty self-referential rhetoric ... and unfortunately this is the typical image of the sommelier to most people. Whereas "explaining" a wine must not be a didactic thing, but rather sharing a story, the story of that particular wine: its territory, its producer, its character and personality. Divulging means putting the interlocutors at ease: the wine tasting experience must be an engrossing, even playful moment, and my task is to involve the guests in an intelligent and hedonistic experience. Of course, under this appearance there must be a profound knowledge of the subject matter, but it does not have to be something like truth revealed. You have to be good, without showing it off—or else, there will always be a barrier of sorts between the sommelier and the guest.

Bracali and the Revolution in Tuscan Cuisine

For the same reason, Luca is not very fond of binge wine tasting. "What is the sense of tasting, say, ten different wines during a meal? Have fewer and enjoy them more. Tasting a good wine must be a slow experience. Take your time, relax. And enjoy every moment of it."

Luca Bracali's search for wines with personality brought him to create his own label. In October 2008 he went to the Champagne region to visit several great wineries—Philipponat, Egly-Ouriet, Selosse and Gaston Chiquet—and meet the producers, in order to select a particular, customized dosage to be commercialized in the restaurant: the bottles had the addition of Bracali's own logo on them. "Previously I had made customized selections from other producers, with my name on it, namely Montevertine, in Radda in Chianti, and Ca' del Bosco, in the Franciacorta area. We got in touch with Gaston Chiquet and there, according to the dosage we wanted, we did a wine tasting in their winery and settled on a particular dosage."

Dosage is the name for a stage near the end of the so-called *methode traditionelle* used for champagne wines: a small dose of sugar (or a blend of wine and sugar syrup) is added to the bottle in order to alleviate the sourness, and it can vary. Hence a variety of denominations which range from the extremely dry ones with less than 3 grams of residual sugar per liter (*Brut nature, Pas dosé, Dosage zero*), to ones with less than 6 grams per liter (*Extra brut*), less than 12 grams (*Brut*), 12–17 grams per liter (*Extra Dry*), 17–32 grams (*Dry*), 32–50 grams (*Demi-Sec*).

Luca Bracali, 2017.

Three—Classicity and Experimentation

Luca reveals,

Personally, I like my champagne with a minimum dosage of sugar. I know it is against the fashion, but it allows the wine to express itself better, and have more personality. And I also needed a more structured wine, that you could drink over the course of a dinner, not as an aperitif. Of course, you need the best possible quality as far as the basic ingredient—grapes—is concerned; for, sometimes, sugar is used to correct a quality that is not excellent in the first place.

Recently I decided to continue the experience, although this time the wine is not labeled as a 'Luca Bracali selection': there is only my name on it, not the producer's. This, because even though I am obviously not a producer, my intervention on these wines was so relevant that they do not taste like the other products from these wineries.

The selections come from three different areas of Tuscany (Bolgheri, San Miniato and Maremma), and they were chosen because of their 'character.' The results are two red wines and a still white wine. Besides selecting the product, Bracali intervened drastically in the production, especially regarding the aging in the winery cellars and the blending of different types of grapes.

They are not *great* wines, mind you. They are not technically impeccable, but they have personality. They are not banal, they are interesting. And I think the result is typically Tuscan.

In my opinion, as a sommelier and wine expert, you have to travel, go to the great wineries, meet the producers, inspect the vines, observe the peculiarities of the territory, immerse yourself in the environment where a wine is born. Or else yours will be a cold, merely theoretical knowledge. It took me twenty years to achieve the knowledge necessary to put my name on a wine bottle. And I don't even remotely think I have reached the maximum knowledge, there is still so much I can learn. And I'm still very, very curious, which I think is the best way to keep learning.

One thing Luca Bracali is very passionate about is the diversity of Tuscan wines, and the importance of making it known to the public.

Basically, of all the wine areas in Tuscany, there are at least four truly great historical ones: Bolgheri, Brunello, Nobile di Montepulciano and Chianti Classico. But within each area, there are many sub-areas, and there can be outstanding differences among the various wineries. Think of Chianti Classico: there is Gaiole, which is quite a cold area, then Radda, then the Southern part, near Castelnuovo Berardenga, which has yet another type of climate.... So, you drink the products by wineries that are at several miles' distance, and taste quite a different type of Chianti Classico. The same goes with Montalcino wines, the climate and terrain makes it for quite different types of wines. The one exception is Bolgheri. Almost all the wines from that area have an absolute elegance and finesse, and Sassicaia is one of the true great wines in the world. These are rational, harmonic wines, I would say "silky"—consistent but light in the mouth. Anyway, back to the diversity—that's the real beauty of it. When speaking about Burgundy, or the Champagne region, this notion is obvious, and widely accepted. Whereas most people think of Tuscany and don't realize the existence of such a variety. It is a continuous discovery, and I feel that this notion must be preserved and communicated, both by the authorities and by those, like us, who do this job. It is an invaluable cultural wealth.

As a maître d,' Luca's vision is quite precise too. "Service is just as important as the dishes you are going to taste. In the collective image, the chef creates an emotion, whereas the front-of-the-house simply brings it to your table. But it is not like that."

The front-of-the-house environment is fundamental, even though nowadays it is very hard to find a good organization in this regard. Sometimes you have restaurants where the chef is brilliant, and the food is excellent, but which nevertheless suffer from a front-of-the-house that is simply not up to the task. Bringing the dish to the table is not simply a mere gesture, but it must be part of a wider concept: hospitality. The dining room must be like an oiled mechanism, and everyone must know his or her tasks to perfection, but there must be also something more: human warmth, and the capacity to make the guest at ease in every moment of the dining experience. "The problem is that nowadays, whereas the media display many model figures for young aspiring chefs, and in a few instances even sommeliers, this does not happen with the front-of-the-house staff," as Luca points out. "I mean, you have hundreds of books about chefs, but how many serious books are there about hospitality in the restaurant?"

And yet, Italian fine dining has a tradition in the field, with such characters as Antonio Santini (of the three-starred Dal Pescatore, in Canneto sull'Oglio, Lombardy), Angelo Valazza (of the two-starred Al Sorriso, in Soriso), Umberto Giraudo (of the three-starred La Pergola, at the Hilton Cavalieri Hotel in Rome). Luca agrees,

These people have made hospitality an art. But they are also complementary to a chef. No matter how brilliant a chef is, there must be someone able to explain the former's philosophy and vision to the guest. What is more, to understand the guest's tastes and interpret them when it is time to choose the dishes from the menu, in order to make the dining experience absolutely perfect, like a custom-made dress. What to do, and what *not* to do. This also helps the kitchen immensely.

This goes beyond the standard requirements, but it is exactly here that hospitality becomes something more than a mere word. At a time when the offer is globalized, the key factors that must stand out are indeed quality and the personalization of the offer itself. This does not mean the maître d' has to be a subordinate, or a servant: he must understand the guest's needs and meet them, without belittling his role.

In France and Great Britain there is a rich tradition regarding the front-of-the house: it is acknowledged a high cultural value, and there are prestigious schools for those who want to become waiters and maître d's. Whereas in Italy—I'm not talking about bars or pizzerias, mind you, but fine dining restaurants—a waiter is very often some young kid who needs to put together some money while he goes to the university. And he does his job mechanically, with no passion or vision—I would even say, without any respect for his own job, because he does not know what it really is, and thinks being a waiter is something humiliating. Which it is not!"

Luca concludes, and then continues,

The same goes with the front-of-the house organization. I don't like restaurants where it is rigidly hierarchic and vertical; this way, the service is usually detached, impeccable but distant. I much prefer a horizontal structure, much like a team-work, with each member of the staff being on the same level. This way, it is undoubtedly more difficult, because it takes a perfect affinity among the various waiters, the maître d,' etcetera. But it works beautifully, and this is how the dining room service worked with Nadia and me. We could understand each other with just one look, and act accordingly. It was like a symphony, with each instrument playing its part in tune with the others. There is room for joking, for having the guests relax and feel like they are with friends. In short, it means enriching the experience.

And it takes skills to be a waiter. It takes sensibility. You have to be a psychologist, and understand your guests in the very first seconds, so as to deal with them in the best possible way—for instance, a foreign guest will have very different demands from an Italian one. You have to know all the technique—the flambage, the decanting, how to serve an oyster, how to portion a duck at the table, how to serve coffee.... And you have to know about the ingredients and raw materials just as much as the chef, because if someone asks a question—a technical question—about a dish, you can't act like a kid who has come to school without learning his lesson! In some ways, it is a continuous challenge. With every new guest showing up at the front door, it is like starting all over again. You see, at a restaurant like ours, guests are supposed to be more than simply people who have come to eat their dinner. They seek a certain complicity, they ask for suggestions, whether it be the wines or the dishes ... in short, they let themselves go, and savor the experience.

When you reach maturity, and a certain experience, you are able to use your knowledge and reevaluate what you have learned, in order to improve upon yourself, day by day. Whereas having a rigid approach can harm the everyday routine in your job, your appreciation of it. But being a waiter is beautiful—it really is.

Behind the Scene, Behind the Stoves: A Day at the Restaurant

Judging from the way the media depict it, a cook's life looks nothing short of wonderful. In these latest years, gastronomy has indeed become the new fad, and the media attention around it has augmented exponentially. Even Italy finally jumped the bandwagon: the Italian edition of the culinary show *MasterChef* cemented the newfound status of Michelin-starred chefs as celebrities. The times of Alberto Sordi greedily devouring a pasta dish while uttering the line *"Maccarone m'hai provocato ... e io me te magno"* (Maccarone, you provoked me ... and I'm goin' to eat ya!") in the cult comedy *Un americano a Roma* (1954, directed by Steno) are long gone. Cooking, in its thousand variations on screen, has become child's play, the edible equivalent of the Lego plastic construction system: You pick random ingredients, turn on the oven and the stove, start the countdown and—*pronto!*—thanks to the magic of television you have created delicious dishes.

Being chef is cool, or at least it looks like it. Sure, in the reality show the young apprentice has to get past the gauntlet of severe masters, who look more like the foul-mouthed sergeants who greet the recruits in war movies and spend the rest of the training shouting at the hapless private's ears and assigning him all types of punishing, humiliating tasks. But it's all part of the game, the price to be paid for the limelight. Creativity, fame, show business. A bit like the young girls who dreams of being dancers, the teenagers who enroll in a hotel management school follow the mirage of celebrity and the goal of the Michelin stars to pin to their chests as if they were medals. But they cannot even remotely imagine the grueling daily restaurant routine. They underestimate the importance of tradition in search of show-stopping effects, and forget the ABC of their job for the benefit of the exploit. Sometimes, they do not even have enough patience to learn how to prepare a gravy. "It took me 30 years to become what I have become today," Bracali explains with a grin. "Whereas nowadays, a young kid who shows up for a stage at the restaurant thinks he can learn everything in *one* year. If only things were that simple...."

Mind you, being a chef can be a wonderful job. But in real life it is quite different than it looks on TV. Even if your restaurant has two Michelin stars. To begin with, the most important aspect, something which neither reality shows nor blogs seem to take into account, are expenses. Providing supplies for the kitchen is a tough job in itself. "The main problem of the restaurants located outside the big cities is that you are forced to make your orders on Monday morning, without knowing what your week will be like," Bracali explains. "Not the least because some ingredients cannot be found easily in the countryside, which is also reflected in the menu." As a result, an urban restaurant can deal with expenses in a safer way, with little waste and the ability to better manage the menu costs. Each dish has its cost, given firstly by the raw materials: foie gras, oysters, langoustine, lobster are obviously far more expensive than vegetables, squab costs more than pork or veal, and so on. A chef who conceives his dishes around "rich" ingredients will necessarily have to sell them at higher prices—unless he cuts on the quality, which is bad. Sure, it is possible to find less expensive lobsters or pigeons, but the end result will not be comparable with the better ones, quality-wise, and every chef worthy of this name knows this by heart.

But the cost is also given by the quantity of the ingredients that have to be purchased for the restaurant supply. For instance, on Mondays Bracali must always order a certain amount of foie gras for the week, based on current bookings (hence one of the reasons why for a restaurant it is so important to have bookings in advance). If all goes well, and during the week there are the expected number of guests, or even more, fine; but it can also happen than, on Sunday evening, after closing the restaurant, in the fridge there is still foie gras in excess, and in that case either you eat it yourself or throw it in the bin. Either way, it is a loss. And the next day you have to order more foie gras for the ensuing week. This also affects the cost of the menu.

Another thing which is perhaps not too clear in the mind of aspiring chefs is the sheer fatigue to be a cook. Such a daily routine was masterfully described by Anthony Bourdain in *Kitchen Confidential*, but on the small screen it is usually softened, smoothed, made user-friendly.

Francesco Bracali's working day starts at 8 a.m., when he arrives at the restaurant. Typically some deliveries have already been made the night before, at the end of the evening shift, even by sending text messages to the greengrocer, but if it is necessary Francesco drives to the market, and selects the products from small farmers.

"The best is the covered market in Follonica, which on the other hand does not always guarantee the same quality of the ingredients, that is one invariable standard," Francesco explains. "Unfortunately I cannot rely on the catch of the day, unlike a seafood restaurant, because on the menu I have several specific dishes, and have to rely on them. I cannot serve a dish to a party of guests on Tuesday, and a different one on Wednesday, of course."

Poultry and game are also supplied once a week: chicken (either

Bracali and the Revolution in Tuscan Cuisine

Bresse or Valdarno: the latter, coming from the Tuscan valley of the same name, is less popular but equally exquisite), pigeon, hare and so on. Fish and seafood are supplied three times a week.

After obtaining supplies, comes the planning for the daily work. "I insist that, each evening, before leaving, each crew member write down what they must do the following day. Each of them has a notebook where they note down each time what they lack to be in line the next day."

"To be in line," in the kitchen jargon, means to ensure that everything needed for a dish is ready at the time a guest orders it. The line planning takes place after the week's last service, so that the next Tuesday, when the restaurant will reopen, all the different aspects of the menu, from sauces to vegetable stock, will be in line. For instance, one thing that has to be prepared anew each week are the flavored oils. Once again, the weekly routine must be organized according to the bookings scheduled for the week, and the orders. Each individual in the kitchen has his own line to follow; if he finishes in advance, he will help someone else, whether it be to bone a chicken, make a gravy, clean the fish and so on.

At a time where chefs are also testimonials for themselves, and spend lots of time in front of the cameras, Francesco Bracali is an exception. He has retained that idiosyncrasy toward outside dictates which characterized him when he was in school. He is able to undergo true marathons in the kitchen, with prohibitive work rhythms, but he is uncomfortable when it comes to fulfilling those obligations that are unavoidable but which he does not "feel."

> My work is primarily in the kitchen, and I rarely stay in the office. I must stay at the stove, cutting, pan-frying, supervising. When I'm in the office I often get lost in a million things and end up not doing what I was supposed to do in the first place.

At 11:30 a.m. and 6 p.m. the brigade eat their meals, all together.

> We have our meals all around the stove, which becomes a table of sorts. It is a convivial moment, we laugh and have fun, and we learn to know each other. In that moment I can get a better idea of the kids who work with me, and who came here at the restaurant to follow their dream. It is also the moment when Luca and I have our arguments, because it is the only moment of the day when we come face to face and have the chance to discuss various subjects.

As in all kitchens, faces and names come and go. Young apprentices stay sometimes for just a few weeks, sometimes for a whole season, before they leave and try to fly with their own wings. Every now and then a stronger bond is formed, which lasts over time. Such was the one between

Francesco and Norio, his Japanese sous chef. Born in 1980, native of Miyazaki, in the Southern part of Japan, Norio Koizumi arrived at the restaurant in 2004, before the big renovation. He had been in Italy for some time, and had worked in Siena. Immediately he and the Bracali brothers got along together very well, and became very close. Norio became like a member of the family. "Even with the inevitable highs and lows, Norio has always been a part of all the vicissitudes of the Bracalis. He called my father "*babbo*" (dad) and my mother "*mamma*" (mom).

In the summer, in the days when the restaurant was closed, we went together to the beach at Follonica, and when Luca and I went dining to a gourmet restaurant, Norio came too. Me, Nadia, Luca and Norio, we were like the four musketeers. There were also arguments, of course, and on those occasions it was hard for me to relate to the Japanese mentality, which in many ways is poles apart from ours."

However, after his long stay in Italy, Norio had become an atypical Japanese. "When he returned to Japan, in 2009, he found it a little uncomfortable.

The Bracali family with a fifth member: Norio Koizumi, Francesco's sous chef, 2004.

His professional and personal growth had been in Italy, in an Italian family." Norio returned in Italy in June 2012, and resumed "his" place in the kitchen. He left again in 2014, to Northern Italy: he became the sous chef at the Enoteca in Canale, the one Michelin star restaurant headed by chef owner Davide Palluda, and eventually returned to his home country.

Junichi Shiba was another Japanese in Tuscany, and during his stay he too became an additional member of the family. Francesco met him at the Ishizaki restaurant, during his promotional tour in Japan in September 2010.

> He began to talk about a subject which I do not care the least bit about—soccer. "Chef, which soccer team are you a fan of?" And when through my interpreter I told him I did not follow soccer, he felt miserable. Of all the Italians in the world, the poor guy had come across one of the few who never, ever liked soccer—a rare bird indeed! And yet, he kept insisting, talking about how after a match, the players from the opposite teams have the habit of exchanging their shirts ... at first I did not understand what he was getting at. And then, through the interpreter and talking with Shiba's Japanese chef, I realized that he had ventured into that speech because he would have liked to have my chef jacket, with my name stitched on it, as a souvenir—and he was too shy to ask me directly!

After his experience in Italy, Shiba returned to Japan, and eventually opened his own restaurant in Tokyo, specializing in his own interpretation of Italian cuisine. The name he chose for it is telling of the deep affection for the two Italian brothers: Shiba called his restaurant "*Bracali*."

Yesterday, Today, Tomorrow

Today Luca and Francesco Bracali's restaurant is a part of the history of Ghirlanda. It is possibly the only motive that pushes people to briefly stop in this small hamlet, before taking a trip up the hill, to the medieval beauties and gorgeous architecture of Massa Marittima. Its anonymous location is not a sight that catches the eye, but its patrons would not change it for any other place in the world.

"I believe we represent a cutaway of Italy which does not accept decadence," Luca Bracali maintains. A decadence caused by many factors. Italy has an enormous wealth—historical, cultural, related to the territory, to its art ... and to its gastronomy as well—which has been dilapidated over the years.

Speaking of gastronomy only, for a tourist who takes a trip to Florence,

Siena or Rome, it is easy to come across tourist traps of all types: taverns, pizzerias or restaurants that offer a terrible approximation of Italian traditional cuisine, with total disregard for raw materials, ingredients, hospitality, attention to the guests ... it is not a matter of prices: even a low-cost tavern should be able to offer at least decent products. Rather, it is very much a matter of lack of culture on the part of the restaurateurs, and indifference to what this job really is about. Who cares about what is on the plate, when the only important thing is business?

"It was never our idea to keep an eye on the calculator," Luca explains. "Since we turned our parents' tavern into a restaurant, we followed our vision, regardless of what it would cost us. The goal was to give more than just good food and wine. We wanted to offer an experience, we wanted to offer emotions." And that is what they did, going against everything to follow their dream. Starting with the location, so far from the usual tourist routes that one must be really motivated to go all the way to Ghirlanda.

Luca Bracali explains:

> The restaurant is located right in front of the old mining station, and it was there for a reason. I think this gives it some sort of historical pregnancy. Not because the station is some sort of beautiful monument—it isn't. But it is a part of our history, it retains the memory of centuries of hard work, it is a symbol of obstinacy and dedication. I like to think that it was not by chance that our restaurant took root just here, at the crossroads. It is symbolic, in a way. And I am proud of this, since nowadays the restaurant is also a reminder of what once was there, for those who can appreciate it. I would like people to discover and understand our history—the history of Ghirlanda, and ours as well—because they are so strictly connected. You have to understand our past in order to know who we are, understand the path we have chosen, and follow us to the future.

A gingham tablecloth, in an overhead view, bedraggled of gravy stains and littered with various objects. A plate with the remains of lunch, a pan with bread slices. A quart of red wine. A grater. The flasks of oil and vinegar. Toothpicks. Crumpled napkins, a cup of coffee, a nutcracker surrounded by shells of peanuts, almonds and pistachios. A pipe, a deck of playing cards, a fly swatter. And a fifty-thousand *lire* note. This is *"Bracali ieri"* (Bracali yesterday). A collage, a three-dimensional snapshot, suspended in time, which has its double in "Bracali today." A mirror image complementary to the former: the same table, the same place, same top-down view. To summarize, however, a completely different restaurant concept. Evolution. A point of arrival.

In *"Bracali oggi"* (Bracali today) the chaotic mess suggested by the earlier work gives way to an image of cleanliness, order, control, refinement: white tablecloths, not jam-packed with objects but with a few symbolic elements, Versace dishes and cups, silver cutlery, a stylish leather notebook, a watch, a cigar, a dish in which a delicacy is placed, characterized by a sensitive, impeccable aesthetic composition. But on the table an odd detail stands out: an overturned glass which soils that immaculateness, to suggest the human presence, give life and vitality to the whole, and close the circle.

For Francesco and Luca Bracali, these two tridimensional collages (created by artists Luca Magdalone and Giulia Capuano) are not merely objects of art to furnish a room of their restaurant. They represent something much more important. They are a way to remember where the two brothers came from, and where they have arrived.

"Wherever I go, I carry a crumb of my past with me," Francesco Bracali likes to say. Between those two works, *Bracali ieri* and *Bracali oggi*, there is an invisible thread which unravels over the years, which is broken and revives, is tangled and thins, then tenses up more and more—strong, neat, decisive. A path through memory, along the course of an entire life.

The story of the Bracali brothers, restaurateurs in Ghirlanda, Massa Marittima, deep in the heart of Tuscany, is a story of hard work and tenacity, disappointment and bad luck, bitterness and success. It is a history of heart and talent, a pure talent that germinates and finds an unexpected outlet in the most unlikely setting amid a thousand difficulties.

This was, and this is, Francesco Bracali. A chef different from any other, and always true to himself. A self that is continually evolving. For him, tomorrow is a range of endless possibilities. A spotless tablecloth on which to write his own future.

Appendix
The World According to Bracali

As it has been noted earlier, Francesco Bracali's cuisine is immediately recognizable at first bite—in fact, even before that, at a glance, by studying its overall harmony and the role of each ingredient. Bracali is one of those chefs who do not need to copy anyone, such is the sheer strength of their own vision.

He synthesizes his idea of kitchen in three key points: to create an enveloping taste; to extract flavors; to enhance the balance—vegetable/animal, fat/acid, sweet/sour, soft/crunchy—in order to create a complete sensorial path. "All my dishes," he explains, "need a millimetrical balance, a conceptual assuredness, and a natural sensibility."

Overall, it is a style that can be defined as maximalist rather than minimalist. On the other hand, the precision, the attention to detail and the use of technique are at the service of the dish itself, and not vice versa. That is, they are necessary to give the ingredients different textures, temperatures etcetera, because for the palate is very important to distinguish and then combine the different sensations and flavors; this way, apparently dissonant elements encounter and blend, creating a unique taste.

More or less, this has always been my goal, but there are many factors that come into play: experience, age, the perfecting of cooking techniques, an interior and professional self-awareness ... all things that in the end affect your vision over the course of time. To me, the most important thing is that behind a dish there must always be a concept, a vision. And it must be well-executed technically, otherwise it won't reflect the chef's idea behind it.

Bracali at work.

Therefore, the chef's technical skills allow him to break free from the slavery of technology and innovative cooking techniques. These, on the contrary, become an instrument to improve upon his ideas, and not an end in itself, because "to let your fantasy loose and look for unusual combinations does not mean to lose touch with territory, seasons and tradition; indeed, it helps to rely on them in a more modern and elegant manner." This is particularly evident when it comes to bringing to new light dishes that are part of the Tuscan or, more in general, of the Italian gastronomic wealth.

A New Take on Tradition, Part One: Spaghetti and Anchovies

An example of the way Bracali filters tradition by way of his own perspective is the *spaghetti con alici* (spaghetti with anchovies). Here, the knowledge of the aliment, inspiration and technique result in a new version of the traditional recipe. It does not necessarily have to be lighter: such a purpose often results in an impoverishment of the overall taste.

On the contrary, the new take on the recipe must enhance the ingredients and bring to mind the original version, but with an additional value. As the chef suggests, "It is as if a light bulb turns on in your brain—the sudden awareness that there can be a completely different way to prepare that dish and reach an even better result." In a way, it is like a rock musician doing a cover version of a classic tune in a personal way, by keeping the basic structure, but reinventing the whole song, the arrangement, the tempo, the mood: think of Jimi Hendrix covering Bob Dylan's "All Along the Watchtower" and making it his own song in the process.

Bracali's reinterpretation of *spaghetti con alici* involves a complex procedure, as customary with the chef. For a start, it features the anchovies in no less than three different ways. The first is a tepid foam of bread, butter and anchovies, which is the basic sauce to be put at the bottom of the plate there. To begin, Francesco prepares a fish soup with small reef and seabed fishes: this is perhaps the core of the recipe, as it enhances the overall flavor. The entire fish is cooked, after removing the entrails. The resulting soup has two parts: a liquid one, which stays on the surface, and another one (so-called *"fondata"*) on the bottom. The latter is passed through a vegetable mill, like Bracali's grandmother used to do with the traditional fish soup used as the basis for *Cacciucco*, the typical Livornese seafood stew.

> I recall my father's mother, sitting on the floor, with this big aluminum vegetable mill in her lap. Its handle was broken, and still is: I have it at home. During cooking the fish literally flaked off and dissolved, so that it was easy to mash it into a soup. Nowadays it would perhaps be easier to use an immersion blender, but conceptually I felt I had to stick to the vegetable mill.

Once again, Tuscan traditional cooking and childhood memory are the starting point of a creation that will move to bold territories.

> Then I toast slices of bread in a rustic manner, in an iron pan, to give the bread a burnt feeling; I put them in a blender with the fish soup and with anchovies in oil from the Cantabrian sea, which are tastier than the ones from the Mediterranean.

Here, sticking to tradition would be pointless, if an improvement can be achieved by choosing better ingredients.

> After blending these elements—anchovies, bread, fish soup—smoothly, I pass them through a strainer to remove any lumps. Then this purée is put into a siphon and siphoned on a plate. The use of siphon gives the resulting foam a light feel, because of the gas bubbles that expand the mixture of ingredients inserted into the siphon. The foam is therefore ethereal, but tasty.

Then it is the turn of the spaghetti, which is stirred with an ultra-smooth purée of raw anchovies—which first must be flash frozen in order to kill bacteria—extra virgin olive oil and fish soup, obtained by putting the mixture into the Pacojet and "pacotized" three times. The use of Pacojet is an example of technique at the service of the concept: due to its precision blade, which shaves a micro-thin layer of the top of a block of deep-frozen ingredients at super-high speed, the Pacojet micro-purees deep-frozen foods into ultra-fine textures (such as mousses, sauces and sorbets) without thawing. This procedure results in the anchovies cooking only when they are stirred with the spaghetti; on the other hand, the "fish soup" purée makes the spaghetti tastier, and on top of that the ferrous, vaguely rancid aftertaste of anchovies is softened.

The dish is finished with the addition of a third type of anchovies (this time raw and marinated), candied lemon peel, wild fennel and toasted bread crumbs. So, in the end, just the basic ingredients are used: anchovies, fennel, lemon, garlic, bread crumbs—nothing else. The recipe is not distorted with the addition of other elements, but the different ways anchovies are employed in the dish enhance the flavor of this traditionally "poor fish," which once could be found only on the tables of fishermen and was barely considered by *haute cuisine*, and give it a new and surprising take. "To me, the most important thing when dealing with a dish that is part of the gastronomic tradition of our country, is not to modernize it, but to *personalize* it."

Bracali is currently considering yet another addition to the dish: an "air" made with *colatura di alici* (anchovy juice). One of the delights of Italian gastronomy, *colatura di alici* is made with anchovies that have been salted and then pressed to release the liquid: it is the modern equivalent of the sauce the Ancient Romans used, called *garum*, a strong and smelly sauce made of fish juice. It has been said, and rightly so, that anchovy juice is "the essence of anchovy more than the anchovy itself." To reinvent this syrupy sauce into an air is yet another step of the chef's brilliant approach to tradition.

A New Take on Tradition, Part Two: The Eel

"*Saòr*," in Venetian dialect, means "*sapore*," taste. And "*Pesce in Saòr*" is a typical Venetian recipe that became one of the most popular ways to prepare fish in Northern Italy. It is as simple as it is delicious: the *pesce in saòr* used to be prepared by fishermen on their boat, in order to solve the problem of preserving fish for many days. The original recipe featured sardines, flour, onion and vinegar, but during the Renaissance a sweet element was added, namely raisins and pine nuts. The sardines are washed under cold water, floured on both sides and then deep-fried in boiling hot oil. The onions are sliced, and sautéed in oil until they become golden, then sugar and white wine vinegar are added. Then layers of fish and onions (plus the pine nuts and raisins) are placed one on top of the other in a glass oven dish, which is put to rest in the fridge for at least 24 hours before serving. There are variations of the same recipe which feature other types of small fish. Bracali decided to use the eel, which is very common in the Veneto and Emilia region, where it is raised in the Delta of the river Po.

"Eels are a fascinating mystery," Bracali explains. "Their reproductive cycle is so complex and mysterious. I still am amazed at the thought that it took hundreds and hundreds of years before man could at least understand its life cycle." Up to the late 18th century, in fact, eel was not even considered a fish: it was an Italian anatomist, Carlo Mondini, who demonstrated it after locating its gonads. A century later, Sigmund Freud spent unfruitful months dissecting eels in search of the male sex organs. And it was not until 1922, when Johannes Schmidt caught eel-larvae in the Sargasso sea, that the first rudiments of European eel's reproductive cycle were put down on paper.

Eels are a gastronomic delight in Italy, although they are consumed mostly in the Northern regions and generally over a limited period, around Christmas holidays—in stew, fried, or marinated in vinegar. In the Po Delta, there are many small taverns where eels are barbecued, a cooking method which results in the leaking of excess fat. Eel is the fish with the highest fat content, over 25 percent, and therefore the most caloric one. It is rich with collagen, has a very elastic skin, and is a very difficult animal to process.

"Frankly, I had trouble killing it," Bracali explains.

One of the bad things about this job is that sometimes you have to do this yourself, and it is not easy if you feel for animals. With eels, it is a horrible thing, and in the past I always tried to avoid it. It was Norio who made me change my mind and give it a try. Eel is a staple in Japanese gastronomy, and they are used to slaughtering the animal. In fact, some procedures that are typical of Japanese kitchen, like *ikizukuri* (live sashimi), are truly grisly, and I personally find them unbearable. The eel must be hanged on a hook, then an incision has to be made all around the head, and the fish must be skinned alive: first the skin must be raised a little, so that it you can grab it with a cloth, as it is very slippery, then it has to be pulled down resolutely. The eel is literally peeled because the skin glides down like a glove. All this, while the poor thing is still moving...

You see, the traditional ways animals were killed for consumption are often very gruesome, certainly not humane. Think of the way the pig was slaughtered by pork butchers...

Norcini (what pork butchers are called in Italy: the name originates from the village of Norcia, in the region of Umbria, from where many of them came) used to tie its back legs and keep it off balance, so that it would fall on the ground and had its throat exposed; then, the *norcino* pierced the animal's chest with a long skewer, searching for the heart. Having been raised in the countryside, for Francesco it was a common occurrence witnessing his grandmother slaughtering rabbits or chickens, but he could never stomach the sight. When dealing with the eel, he tried to make the slaughtering as brief and humane as he could.

With the eel there have two be two of us at work, one doing the cut, and the other wearing gloves, or with the hands covered with coarse salt, so as to be able to hold the fish still in spite of the slippery substance all over the skin. But I just couldn't get myself to skin the poor thing alive. So, I have a crew member keep the animal still, then I just cut off its head and that's it. I try to fillet it in the fastest way possible, but the macabre thing is, the body keeps moving for a while.

After being filleted, the eel must rest in the fridge for at least one night, or better still a whole day. This way, the texture becomes apt for cooking. As with all animals, there is the need for chilling the meat. Then, the next day the eel is steam cooked with orange and lemon peel, pot herbs and peppercorns, so that the skin becomes as smooth and tender as possible, and loses its elasticity. Even more importantly, with steam cooking the meat loses most of its fat. Then I cut it into small pieces and store it up. When a guest orders the dish, the pieces of steamed eel are immersed in a tempura and deep fried.

This way, the meat undergoes three passages: the chilling, which helps its fibers and skin relax and acquire a softer texture; steam cooking; and, finally, deep frying. The result is crunchy on the outside but has an extremely soft texture, while the taste retains a personality, as well as the eel's typical earthy aftertaste.

Bracali's version features all the traditional ingredients of the *saòr* recipe: red onion, salt, raisins, sugar, vinegar. But these elements are reinvented in different, unexpected ways. For instance, the vinegar becomes a thin film.

I created a water and vinegar solution, made in a two-part process. First I boiled it with agar-agar for a very short time; agar-agar is a very interesting gelling agent, but in order for it to activate, it must be boiled in liquid, and so freshness and acidity get lost in the process. So I added more water and vinegar in order to keep the original acidity, and spread it over a plate: what I obtain is a thin layer of this gel-like vinegar solution that I will add to the dish.

As for the other elements, I prepare an onion ice cream which I put on top, while raisins are added as dressing together with a sautéed seasonal vegetable, like zucchini, asparagus, turnip greens. This vegetable element is necessary to balance the dish. My own addition to the recipe is the sapid, creamy sauce at the bottom of the plate, which is made with Cinta senese *lardo* (smoked by me). This is the element which brings together the different parts, and creates the 'enveloping taste.' So I have savoriness, crunchiness, acidity; the taste of eel is enhanced, but the onion ice cream adds freshness and sweetness to it, as in the traditional recipe, and the accompaniment of vegetables and raisins balances the whole.

As in the previous recipe, first comes the distinction of the various ingredients, and the analysis of their function; then comes the reassembling, under a new perspective. But another important step, and not one to underestimate, is to find the right way to serve the dish to the guests, so that they can appreciate the overall result. Francesco wants his food to speak for itself.

I don't like having to "explain" the dish as if in school, and "teach" the correct way to eat it. I believe that if a dish has a strong concept behind it, it must also be presented in the correct way by the chef so that whoever is going to eat it will be able to appreciate it for what it is. In short, the dish must be presented in the best possible way for the guest to taste it, and each bite must contain the various elements. Eating must be a simple action, not a matter of "First you taste this, then you add a little bit of that, but be careful not to forget that other element..." you know?

Working on the Raw Materials: The Chianina Beef Tartare

Bracali's quest for top-notch raw ingredients resulted in his teaming up with Simone Fracassi. Since 1927 the Fracassi family has had a famous butcher's shop in Rassina, Castel Focognano, in the Casentino region, in the province of Arezzo. This part of Tuscany is famous for the Chianina cattle: one of the oldest breeds of cattle, the Chianina originated in the area of Valdichiana (hence its name) and has been raised for more than 2200 years. Formerly a draught breed, now it is raised mainly for its beef, in Tuscany, Umbria and Lazio. Chianina oxen are a sight to behold. They were described by the Latin agriculture writer Columella as "*vastos et albos"* (huge and white), and rightly so: the males weigh up to 1,500 kilograms and stand up to 5 ft. 11 inches tall (the castrated males may reach 6 ft. 7 inches). With a growth rate of 4.4 lbs. per day, Chianina cattle are a strong breed, with high tolerance of heat and sunlight, and give a nutritious, exceptionally flavored meat, which is sold by name by approved butchers. Chianina meat is mainly used for the *Bistecca alla fiorentina* (beefsteak, Florentine style), one of the signature dishes of Tuscan cuisine: it is grilled over a wood or charcoal fire and then seasoned with salt, pepper and olive oil, in large cuts which must usually be shared between two or more persons. It is served *"al sangue"* (very rare) and must be accompanied with a good Chianti wine. Due to its tenderness, flavor and digestibility, the Chianina meat is also delicious when served rare, finely chopped as a steak tartare.

Simone Fracassi is the ambassador of Chianina beef in the world. According to his philosophy, he carefully selects the best locally-reared breed from nearby farms, and prioritizes quality above all else. He also selects the finest Cinta Senese porks for cold cuts, and to many his ham is the best in Italy.

Bracali met Fracassi in 2015. He took a trip to the latter's small butcher's shop and spent a whole day there to personally meet the man and taste his products. On the other hand, Bracali's bold approach to Tuscan cuisine and original style caught Fracassi's interest immediately. The following year, Fracassi invited Bracali to participate in his annual food and wine event *"Capolavori a Tavola,"* (Masterpieces on the Table) which has taken place in the medieval village of Poppi since 2001, and the chef decided to present his own interpretation of the Chianina.

You see, beef tartare is often considered an "easy" dish, whereas it is actually quite a difficult one. Eating Chianina beef tartare in restaurants, I often found some flaws. Firstly, the meat texture was too strong, and this was a problem concerning the type of meat used, which was not of the optimal quality, or slaughtered too hastily. On other occasions, my palate perceived a texture as if the meat had been pre-chewed, possibly the result of an incorrect processing of the meat itself; sometimes an incorrect chopping can result in the meat literally flaking off. Another characteristic that did not convince me was that the sauces which accompanied the meat were often too intrusive, and did not enhance the main ingredient—on the contrary, they stood above it, so much so that the Chianina's delicate flavor was often lost.

Having become aware of that, I set out to study and think over the problem, taking up also the notions that Simone transmitted to me. Firstly, I thought about a sauce to dress the tartare, which had to be tasty but not aggressive. And what I came up with is neither a "sauce" in the true sense of the term nor a flavored oil: I use soy sauce, garlic-flavored oil (which I have prepared in advance), sweet-and-sour sauce—and absolutely no salt. The procedure is not easy at all, as you can see: first thing in the morning I have to prepare the flavored oil, cooking it at the right temperature with five garlic cloves in it; as soon as it begins to fry slightly, I take it off the stove and leave it for the remainder of the day; meanwhile I prepare the sweet-and-sour sauce in another small pan, using white vinegar and sugar. Then I put together five spoonfuls of flavored oil, two spoonfuls of sweet-and-sour sauce and two spoonfuls of soy sauce, I toast the sesame seeds and add them to the mixture. I marinate it overnight with toasted sesame seeds, drain it, and the concentrated liquid I obtain—only one spoonful of it—is the sauce with which I will dress the meat.

It took a while to balance the various components of this sauce, which was born as an outside dressing, whereas now I mix it with the chopped meat while massaging it. But the idea itself came quite quickly, because of my 'mental palate' which allowed me to figure out the final taste in advance. I knew I had to add flavor to the meat without being obtrusive, so I could not use any salt at all, as it is too invasive. The soy sauce itself had to be of the right type, and not too savory: as with balsamic vinegars, there are many different types, more or less salty.

Then I portion the meat, chop it finely with the knife, and add the sauce I prepared. I mold it into little meatballs and then I start massaging it. Passing these little balls of meat from one hand to the other has the effect of slightly warming the meat and releasing its collagen, which remains on the outside. This way, the tartare acquires a more complex texture, which is more satisfying to the palate: the exterior is smoother and acts as a bonding agent, whereas the interior maintains the typical texture of Chianina beef and enhances it. This way, it is as if I have divided the meat into two parts, one which is processed and one which is not, but which are still part of the same whole.

The idea of massaging the meat hints at the overstressed stories about the treatment done in Japan to the Wagyu Tajima cattle, to produce the Kobe beef. The farmers would allegedly massage the live animals daily, sometimes with sake, as a proxy for exercise in the tight living quarters and to further accentuate the marbling that Kobe beef is so well known for.

The accompanying dressing on the plate is a very light mayonnaise, made with water, oil and chive; the acid part, which the mayonnaise is lacking, is given by little mounds of dried raspberry scattered on the plate. The dish is served with pot herbs and wild flowers. The pot herbs I use are 'frail' ones, that is wild fennel, dill, basil—whereas the 'hard' pot herbs are rosemary, laurel, sage—whose consistency is more apt to the dish. Here, again, my childhood memories find a way into the dish itself: when I was a kid, I used to go and pick up edible wild herbs for the salad with my grandma, in the countryside area around Ghirlanda: chicory, rampions, dandelions...

The result shows an in-depth study of the raw material and its qualities, and goes beyond the standard beef tartare that is so common in fine dining restaurants, where often it is assumed that good quality meat, extra virgin olive oil and salt are all that is necessary to have a good beef tartare dish.

Usually, the idea is that you can't go wrong with those basic ingredients, since in Tuscany we have them in their finest quality. I had a somewhat different perspective. To me, it was a matter of valorizing Chianina meat, and caressing it—literally, with the manual massaging, and symbolically, with the choice of the right accompanying flavors. Of course, the starting point had to be a top-notch quality beef, and Simone Fracassi was the only one who could guarantee me that. My task was to give personality to this excellent product—like finding the perfect make-up for a beautiful actress. The dried raspberry and the other herbs and flowers add a further complexity, because with every bite you can have a slightly different aftertaste, given by this or that vegetable element. So, the result is something that gives you an idea of Fracassi's products and Bracali's vision.

Bracali employs the same concept to his shrimp tartare, a new dish of the 2018 menu. The dish is a new take on an old Bracali creation, the mortadella ravioli with a shrimp tartare on a cream of borlotti beans. The shrimps are dressed with passion fruit instead of lemon (as the former is

The Chianina beef tartare, in the restaurant.

equally acid but less aggressive to the palate than the latter), some drops of soy sauce, extra virgin olive oil and a pinch of salt, and served with a mortadella of Prato foam (mortadella of Prato is a Tuscan variation of the typical mortadella sausage from Bologna with the addition of pounded garlic) and puffed *polenta* chips with cumin.

> The original idea was to use pistachios instead of cumin, in order to have a common element with mortadella, which is normally flavored with pistachios. There was a problem, though. First I have to prepare the *polenta*, then spread it in order to make it very thin, veil-like, put it between two sheets of silpat, and put it to dry. When it has completely dried, it is broken in pieces manually, and puffed up in a pan, for several seconds, in hot oil. The risk is that other ingredients can burn, and whereas cumin powder can be added later, after puffing up the polenta, this is not possible with pistachio.

A Return to the Origins: Making Bread

The wild gastronomic diversity of Italy is reflected in the bread, as every region has its own different types, in addition to those that are typical all over Italy. Bread can be flat or puffed up, soft or dried, with a soft or hard crust, white or dark.... It can be made with different types of flour, and enhanced with everything: sesame seeds, fennel seeds, olives, raisins, onion, small bits of bacon, cheese and ham. The typical Tuscan bread has an important characteristic: it is made without salt. The reason for this dates back to the Middle Ages, when salt was heavily taxed: to cut costs, bakers went without, and the tradition stayed even after the tax was lifted.

Tuscan bread is pale-looking and pale-crusted, at the first bite bland-tasting for someone who is used to the typical salty bread. In fact, this particular taste makes it much more delicate, and a perfect accompaniment to cold cuts and cheese, as well as to dipping into the thick sauces that form a basic part of the regional cuisine—not to mention its role in some of Tuscany's key dishes, such as the *crostini* (where it is grilled or toasted and served with chicken liver pâté), the tomato *bruschetta* (where it is brushed with extra virgin olive oil, grilled or toasted, and spooned with a tomato, oregano and garlic mix), and the *pappa al pomodoro*.

As many other colleagues did, during the first years at the restaurant Francesco Bracali offered the bread in the form of various flavored rolls, served warm at the beginning of the meal, in order to quench the appetite. Then he started thinking that in the past bread had another purpose: to merely accompany the meal. Although delicious, the flavored rolls were something different in concept than bread, and as such they were superfluous, if not even detrimental; the guests ended up satiated too early, and did not appreciate the latter part of the meal, when the main courses are served. So, he had to recreate a balance, and give bread its original function. This meant abandoning small rolls in favor of large loaves of bread, presented to the guests on a bread trolley, then sliced and served during the meal. It was, in a way, a return to the origins, to a time when bread was a symbol of basic nourishment.

Another key element in developing a new concept regarding the use of bread at his restaurant was Francesco's childhood memories: he recalled when, as a kid, his grandmother used to make bread once a week. The bread was kept under a slightly moistened cloth inside the cupboard, and maintained its softness for the whole week.

> Here, without having read up in any way, I started realizing the importance of making bread. The bread I recalled as a kid was more compact, and had a smaller alveolation. Nowadays, when you go and buy your bread at the bakery or at a supermarket, most of the times you notice that it has a thin crust and a pronounced alveolation, which gives it a sense of lightness. And yet, the next day, this bread is already stale, and as hard as a brick. Over time I realized that this kind of alveolation is not normal, because the bread has been made with the addition of leavening agents to aid the raising process, and have it take place in a shorter time.

So, why did his grandma's bread keep its original consistency for one week whereas now it lasts only one day? The most important thing was to understand how to make a bread as light and digestible as possible. On the one hand, Bracali decided to use only certain types of flour. Nowadays it has become fashionable to rediscover ancient types of grain, as well as the procedure of grinding between stones, as it used to be in the old days. "It is a positive thing, indeed, because we were all used to types of flour that were even too refined and in fact lost a large part of their original flavor." An important factor in the making of bread is the type of flour which is used. As with all long levitations, a "strong" or "hard flour" is needed, with a higher gluten content than the "weak" or "soft flour." "Personally, I like a flour which keeps at least a 30 percent of bran, which gives flavor and smell to bread, and adds that toasted feeling to the crust."

This led also to another decision: after doing research on baker's yeast Bracali set out to create his own "*lievito madre,*" that is the sourdough starter which by now has been abandoned amongst professional bakers but was the core of baking tradition in Italy.

To create the *lievito madre*, Francesco grated an apple and added flour and mineral water to it. "I used the Perrier mineral water, because it is a highly carbonated water." He kept it for 48 hours in a jar, at room temperature and with the lid placed loosely: for live organisms to form, that is the yeast and microbacilli, it must be exposed to air. "After 48 hours, you notice that this almost gaseous part has formed. When you smell it, it has a pungent odor, a bit like the one you sense when you scratch the head of a match."

After obtaining the sourdough starter, Francesco started to refresh it, in order to maintain and feed it, and keep it healthy. "At a certain point, the dough falls asleep and dies if it is not fed properly: it means it is not active, and does not work as a leavening agent. By refreshing it, you practically feed it with new flour and water, and allow it to regenerate."

The refreshments are done with the same quantity of flour and yeast, and 50 percent water. It takes at least four to six refreshments for the pre-dough (or "*biga*") to be ready. Between one refreshment and the other, at the beginning, at least four to six hours must pass, and the process must take place at room temperature. "With each refreshment, you must throw away a part of it, to keep the dough healthy: for instance, if I have 700 grams of sourdough, after each refreshment I throw away 200 grams and keep the other 500." Then the sourdough is put in the fridge and refreshed from time to time, depending on how frequently one uses it.

Working with sourdough requires attention and responsiveness. To keep the *lievito madre* in ideal condition, one must understand its processes, keep an eye on its color, smell and consistency, and act in one way or the other whenever it is needed.

The beautiful thing about sourdough starter is that it is *alive*. It is a beautiful feeling, to create something out of nothing, by using basic elements—flour, water, and the acidic element of the grated apple. And you learn how to feed it and make it grow when you manipulate it, regardless of all the notions you have learned at school or in books. It is a living thing, and it changes according to humidity and temperature; consequently, the doughs you make with it will change too. For instance, the bread you make from the *lievito madre* on August 15 will be different from the one you make in mid–December, since the acidity will be different, etcetera. So, you have to be careful with these factors as well.

Francesco elaborates on assessing the needs of the dough.

The sourdough must be vigorous, and sometimes it tends to lose strength, for there are many factors that influence it in different ways. For instance, if you don't refresh it for a while its enzymes are going to die, giving it a color, smell, taste and consistency that are not good: the taste will be too acidic, the color too dark ... in this case, when you refresh it you must add less yeast and more flour and water, in order to recover the previous balance. On the other hand, when the temperature is too cold, the sourdough starter needs a "push," in two ways: either with an alcoholic agent, or a lactic one. For instance, you can add a spoonful of natural yogurt, which has its own enzymes and bacteria. Whereas, since I created the sourdough starter with fruit, I use sultana raisins, which I put in a jar with water in a warm spot, near the stove, in order for the grapes to release an acidic liquid, rich with bacteria and enzymes. This liquid gives strength to the sourdough starter when it has become too "light," that is when it has lost its strength.

The baking procedure (so-called "indirect method") which starts with a pre-dough—the *"biga"* (less hydrated) or *"poolish"* (more hydrated)—made with sourdough starter, is much longer and more complex, but the bread has a perfect alveolation, very different from the one made with brewer's yeast (direct method), or with the semi-direct method, when the dough is obtained by mixing all the ingredients together in a single step and later adding the yeast that can be natural or more often chemical. The molds take root less easily in an acid environment and this is one of the reasons why bread made with the starter lasts longer.

Sourdough bread is also much more digestible, as Francesco explains,

Unlike what most people believe, this digestibility is given mostly by the yeasts and bacteria that sourdough starter accumulates. When they come into contact with the acidic enzymes of saliva, they activate the process of digestion immediately. This means that when you eat standard bread, you chew and swallow it, and then wait for the stomach acid to attack the food, and as you know about 50 per cent of it is secreted during this phase; with bread made with sourdough starter, a pre-digestion takes place already in the mouth during the chewing process. Moreover, you won't feel thirsty afterwards. So, by helping boosting digestion considerably, this type of bread is a lot healthier.

To Preserve and to Treasure: Onion Cappuccino

The onion cappuccino was born after Bracali's meeting with a young farmer who was also a *"Coltivatore custode"* (Custodian grower). Mass selection, as carried out by the farmers over the centuries, has led to the definition of many local varieties able to make the best of the natural resources of a multitude of habitats. Today, these old varieties are often at the risk of extinction, and this is why the figure of the custodian grower was born. Custodian growers work closely with the Tuscan germplasm bank, and have been selected based on criteria aimed at the conservation of local varieties and breeds at risk of extinction. Fifty-eight growers were selected in the early 2000s, and enrolled in a special list: they are followed constantly by special technicians, and must satisfy three aims: they must reproduce *in situ* (that is, on farm) the seeds conserved at the Regional germplasm bank, as a way to "renew" conserved seeds; they set up a conservation system of the local varieties at risk of extinction; they must permit the recording of the main morphological characters by selected personnel from ARSIA (the Regional Agency for the Development and Updating of Agriculture and Forestry Programs).

Therefore, custodian growers carry out specific tasks: they oversee the safety of the single genetic resources, protecting and safeguarding them from any and all forms of contamination, alteration or destruction; they spread knowledge about the cultivation of the genetic resources of which they are custodian; they carry out renewal of the seeds of herbaceous species conserved in the Regional germplasm bank. These growers

The Onion Cappuccino.

are often the only holders of knowledge about the techniques linked to the cultivation or use of the local varieties. Such a cultivation is more expensive than the modern standard techniques: it needs more labor, more cropping operations, and results in a lower productivity, or a lack of market for the products. To support the cost needed to maintain the "on farm" cultivation, the region provides them with a minimal reimbursement.

Custodian growers are often located in mountainous areas, where intensive agriculture is nearly impossible, and theirs is a labor of love and passion; with their existence, they nevertheless have raised an interest on the part of local institutions, resulting in a number of projects dedicated to the valorization of local products. Some of these include the chestnuts for "Farina di Neccio" PDO in Garfagnana, the "Valle di Chio" cherry, the "Canestrino" tomato from Lucca, the "Fagioli della Lucchesia" beans, the Bigliolo beans, the fruit and garden species of Valtiberina, Casentino and Garfagnana, the pears from the Dalla Nave alla Cicogna Botanical Park near Arezzo, and the "Treschietto" onion. The latter was the product that Bracali chose to work on.

Small and round, characterized by pink color and a sweet flavor, this onion is typical of the Lunigiana area, and is grown between November and December. Due to its delicate, light taste, it can also be eaten raw, but its layers have a rather strong texture, and even after a prolonged cooking they maintain this almost 'meaty' consistency. Bracali cooks it in a very simple way, with salt, pepper and extra virgin olive oil, almost exclusively in the onion's own water; this, until it has become tender. Sometimes he adds vegetable broth. There is no searing. Then he adds egg and creates a foam, which is put in a siphon, kept in water bath and then siphoned in a teacup, resulting in a *"cappuccino"* of sorts.

On top of it, instead of cocoa, the chef puts small crumbles of Cinta Senese *guanciale* (pork cheek) which he has first sautéed in a pan so as to make it crunchy, and a few drops of 25-year-old Balsamic vinegar—so syrupy it is almost a sauce, rather than a vinegar. The harmony and complexity of the vinegar give the dish a kick. "I put exactly five drops of it, one in the middle and the others around, so that for every spoonful there will be one drop of vinegar, thus creating the exact taste balance I want, without having to tell the guest what is the correct way to eat it—this, in my opinion, is part of a chef's intelligence in creating a dish."

The cappuccino is served with a slice of homemade brioche bread, which is briefly sautéed in an iron pan to achieve a slightly toasted, rustic flavor. It perfectly blends with the cappuccino foam and creates a fascinating game of mirrors, so to speak, with the sweet element given by the onion, and the acid complexity of the vinegar. Here, a minimum of ingredients results in an extremely refined dish, and the best way to enhance such a "poor" ingredient as onion.

Playing with Technique: Strawberry Grape Caviar

One of Bracali's signature creations is the nettle gnocchi on a foie gras pudding, a strawberry grape caviar and dried fruit—a superlative dish, which, to quote Enzo Vizzari, shows admirably "the chef's top-notch virtuosity, in the encounter between dissonant elements." (*L'Espresso*, July 17, 2014.) Such an admirable balance is achieved with a scientific precision worthy of pastry, because just a slight predominance of this or that element would be enough to mess up a perfect mosaic. Because, as Francesco explains, "the right balance of flavors is crucial for the success of a dish, and the chef's ability consists in finding such balance, always and in any case. This is possible only if the ingredients are skillfully linked together by an ideal logical thread."

The gnocchi are made with dried nettle powder, red potatoes and potato flour; they are stirred in with sour butter and Parmesan cheese, with the addition of broth to create a creamy feel enhanced by the starch that comes out of the gnocchi. On the bottom of the plate we have a foie gras pudding, similar to a *crème royale* and made with foie, cream and egg yolk, inspired by Joël Robuchon's recipe.

> I spread a thin layer of it and put it in the steam oven for four or five minutes; after drying the plate I put the gnocchi over the pudding, then I add a dried fruit powder and a caramelized onion powder on top—this because I did not want to put other ingredients in the gnocchi nor make another sauce, but wanted to add a further nuance which only a powder would allow. Finally, I add a mound of strawberry grape caviar and fried nettle leaves for decoration.

A key element in the dish is the caviar made with Isabella grape. This quality (known as *Vitis labrusca*, or American grape) has a very particular smell, which some compare to strawberry (hence the name strawberry grape, under which it is also commonly known). It was brought to Europe in the 1800s, and is historically blamed as the American grape variety that carried the phylloxera plague, microscopic fly-like insects that destroyed most of Europe's wine-producing vines. American phylloxera-resistant rootstocks were subsequently imported to Europe so that European vines could be grafted on and survive.

Isabella grape is used to make a sweet and refreshing ruby-colored sparkling wine, the so-called *Fragolino*. Nowadays Fragolino is not considered a wine any longer, since the term is reserved for the products of fermentation of European grape, or *Vitis vinifera*: its commerce was banned in 1979 within the EEUU, officially because it is difficult to control the level of methanol produced during fermentation, which can be poisonous. Therefore, strawberry grapes are mostly used for table, and in Tuscan gastronomy they are a key ingredient of the traditional *schiacciata con l'uva*, a flat bread with grapes. It is made from the normal *schiacciata*, flat bread (like a thick pizza crust) and then covered with grapes, about 5 pounds of sugar, and baked; it is yet another demonstration of the way traditional specialties evolved out of necessity, as farmers could not afford "rich" food and had to eat whatever they could.

Bracali's idea was to use spherification in order to add an element to the nettle gnocchi.

That's what I mean when I talk about putting your knowledge at the service of the dish. I needed something fresh to add on top of the gnocchi; it must not melt, and had to be distributed uniformly, so it was a difficult issue. The idea came to me of using agar-agar; unlike other gelling agents, though, you need to boil it in liquid to use it. For example, if I have to prepare a passion fruit jelly, when using isinglass I only have to heat up a minimal quantity of passion fruit, melt isinglass in it and add the rest of the fruit juice later. This way, I obtain an almost natural jelly. With agar-agar, this is not possible: I have to heat passion fruit almost to boiling point, say 185°F, in order to melt agar-agar in it. As a result, the fruit loses its freshness and naturalness.

The idea of using strawberry grapes was once again the result of childhood memories. When my parents worked at the gas station, next to it there lived an elderly couple who used to help my dad. There was a garden behind the house, where they cultivated a small row of vines. It was strawberry grape. Every now and then, in the summer, this elderly lady used to call me and offer me some grapes. We used to eat grapes on a slice of bread as a snack, from mid–August to mid–September— no junk food, no industrial prepackaged snacks, it was healthy and so delicious!

Bracali spin-dried the grape and obtained a juice, which had a tannin element given by the peel. This rather fastidious taste had to be eliminated. He added a 10 percent of sugar and heated it up to 185°F.

The foam that forms over the liquid has the same effect as when clarifying a broth—that is, all the impurities come to the surface. Then the result is filtered through a cloth and what you have is an extremely limpid liquid which nevertheless has all the characteristics of strawberry grape, the same taste and smell.

I make this juice at a certain time of the year, when the grapes are ripe, then I have to blast chill it and keep it stored. But I can heat it up again whenever I want, and add agar-agar for the spherification, and it never loses its freshness. It is basically the same procedure as when making a sorbet—instead of heating it up, I could put it in the Pacojet, and have a strawberry grape sorbet instead. Whereas for making the caviar, I add 0.8 to 1 gram of agar-agar for every 100 grams of strawberry grape juice, and put it in a large surgical syringe (without the needle, of course). Then I drop down drop after drop in a bowl with cold seed oil. When the drop touches the oil, it turns into a sphere and falls to the bottom of the bowl.

He then drains the bowl, rinses the spheres in water, dries them: "There you have the caviar."

Opulence and Tastefulness: His Majesty, the Pigeon

Roast chicken is a signature Sunday dish in many Italian families. Bracali employs the Valdarno chicken: its hind legs are particularly big, muscular and strong, whereas the breast is lean. These chickens, being raised on a farm, must go around looking for food, and go back in the hen-house only for resting. Francesco explains the difference,

Chickens that have a shelter made with straw and a canopy to protect them from rain, grow in a more natural environment than farmed batteries, of course. They get used to the different temperature between day and night, and form their own antibodies. To make a quick example, it is like children who grow up in the countryside, in a farmhouse: they stay in open air, make daily exercises, eat good healthy food etcetera. They normally grow healthier and stronger than kids who stay all day in their city flat and never put their nose out, eat junk food and watch TV all day. You know what I mean?

It is not enough to rely on top-notch products: one must also know how to choose the ones that suit his cooking style best. The same goes with the pigeon. Like many of his colleagues, Bracali orders pigeons from Longino & Cardenal. However, he prefers the *etouffé* one: not slaughtered and bled to death, but suffocated. This way, the blood remains inside the animal and gives the meat a sweeter flavor, juicy and firm. The squab is accompanied with a sauce of carrots and chocolate, which blends together the sweet vegetable element with a bitter note, and with a mushroom risotto.

But chickens, pigeons and other birds have to be cooked properly. Cooking which technically features an issue: how to cook the thigh correctly without overcooking the breast, and keep the meat tender while keeping the skin crunchy. For instance, chicken breast is almost devoid of fat and rich with protein, and this is why it is a staple in the diet of athletes and people who want to lose weight. On the other hand, the thigh has a much different texture and composition. Chicken, pheasant, pigeon, partridge, are traditionally cooked as a whole, roasted in the oven or skewered on the spit. "This way, though, when the breast was cooked correctly, the thigh resulted undercooked, almost raw, and vice versa: when the thigh reached its cooking point, the breast was already overcooked, tough and stringy." Given the different texture of muscles and nerves in the thigh, the animal must be cooked in two different ways.

When we are supplied with pigeons, the carcasses and wings are used for the gravy. The thighs are vacuum packed with sage, rosemary, garlic, salt and pepper, and are cooked at low temperature (154°F) for four hours. The breast is left intact, but is separated from the fillet, that small slice under the main portion of the breast, just above the ribcage, around the center of the sternum. The fillet is put aside, raw. Then, when someone orders the dish, we take the breast, marinate it with extra virgin olive oil and a special mix of herbs for 10–15 minutes. Then the breast is pan-fried, almost exclusively on the side of the skin, in order to make it crunchy, and then turned around for about one minute, near the end, so that the herbs don't burn and the heat penetrates inside gradually.

The breast is then left to rest for a bit; this way, the juices that concentrated inside the breast during the searing, when the meat pores were sealed by the heat, expand all over again throughout the portion. This is important for two reasons, concerning taste and health: it is wrong to slice a piece of meat immediately after it has been cooked, because this way the juices will come out and the meat will lose an essential, healthy part of its flavor and essence. Whereas, by letting it rest, the meat will preserve all these juices, and be tastier and healthier. The breast must therefore remain pinkish, tender and slightly bloody.

At this point, it is time to "finish" the thigh. Vacuum cooking the meat makes it tender, but a bit uniform in texture, a bit like as if it had been boiled, whereas the inside must be tender, and the outside a bit crunchy. To give it a roasted flavor, I place it in the salamander for a while: this broiler unit has an extremely high temperature overhead that gives the skin the required crispy effect. As for the fillet, it would be a pity to cook it. So, I serve it raw, as a tartare, seasoned with the same mix of herbs. Whereas the gravy made with the carcass and wings is used to stir up the mushroom risotto.

Many guests are delighted by the exquisite carrot and chocolate sauce, an unusual and surprising blend of flavors. But Bracali is particularly proud of the mix of herbs, a "hidden" part of the recipe which nevertheless gives it an extra touch.

It took me almost two years to find the right balance. Generally, in supermarkets you find packed roasting herbs, but I wanted to create my own. I started by drying different ingredients: sage, rosemary, onion, garlic, lemon peel, thyme, capers and salt. I cut the garlic into thin slices, and dried it; took the rosemary needle-like leaves and dried them; and so on. Once dried, I blended every single ingredient in the coffee grinder. Then I took a precision scale, like the ones goldsmiths use, and started calibrating the different ingredients, until I finally reached a satisfying mix: 6.2 grams of dried garlic powder; 4.5 grams of dried rosemary powder; 2 grams of dried lemon peel; 5 grams of dried onion powder; 5 grams of dried caper powder; 2 grams of dried thyme powder; 2.3 grams of salt; 2.5 grams of sugar. It is the result of endless trial and error, and I have always been very jealous of it. This formula is one of the few things I have never talked about either when teaching cooking classes, with colleagues or journalists. I perfected a similar mixture for the pork, with the addition of elements with a watery part, such as powdered olives and tomatoes, which was even more difficult to balance.

The Pigeon.

119

The result is nothing short of outstanding. It has been described by the eminent Enzo Vizzari as "a work of art ... the boost—expected, but more insinuating, progressive, than violent—reaches the palate after the encounter between the meat and the sauce; if not the best ever, certainly at the top among the hundreds of pigeons tasted in the memory of the militant gourmet.

Observation and Reinvention: The Squid Chocolate

Bracali's creative taste for combinations is still fertile, but compared with the past there are no wrong notes. The dishes have reached a millimeter balance, and a strength in concept and taste which is often stunning. This is evident even in the moments of transition, in the small divertissements between one course and he next. Such is the squid chocolate, a creation born almost by accident, and an example of how invention arises from spirit of observation combined with creative reworking.

The idea came to me while preparing a bisque with the shells of shrimp. I had put the vegetable to brown, and then put the shells on another pan, with oil, to which I would add liquor and white wine. At some moment I noticed that the shells were releasing their pigment, and colored the oil with a bright orange tint. At this point I stopped to think about the possibility of obtaining a coral-colored oil, or better still an overlay. I did a test with clarified butter instead of oil: I had the shrimp shells brown on the pan, whipped them and then passed them through a sieve. The result was almost identical as before, but kept a vague butter-like flavor, whereas I needed a fat that, once solidified, had a more neutral taste. And so I thought of cocoa butter, which I use to make chocolates as well as a pre-dessert called *cioccobanana* (cocoa-banana). I thought I could create something similar to a chocolate, but salty, with an overlay obtained from the pigment of the shrimps. So I put the shells to dry in the oven, and then I toasted them in the pan with cocoa butter. The shells dried and released the pigment which is inside them, with no watery part. I hereby melted it all, whipped the melted cocoa butter and the shell shrimps, which crumbled like dust, and passed the result through a sieve, thus obtaining an orange-colored butter. Good, now let's see if the overlay works, I thought. I took an ice cube—I needed something cold to dip into the butter—and dipped it briefly. The butter covered the submerged part perfectly, and formed a glaze immediately: cocoa butter had solidified instantly and created a thin and homogeneous layer.

So, I started from the outside, from the layer. Now I must think about the filling. I decided to remain on ingredients from the sea, and opted for cuttlefish, which I cooked at a low temperature for a long time in order to soften it. Once cooked, I cut it and put it into circular-shaped molds which I then froze, so as to obtain one centimeter tall cylinders. Then, with a long stick, I pierced the cuttlefish cylinders and dipped them into the melted cocoa-and-shrimp butter a couple of times, until the cylinder was completely covered by this thin shrimp-flavored layer, and looked indeed like a chocolate. Then I put everything back in the refrigerator, so that the inside of the chocolate would be cold but not frozen. When served to the guests, the cuttlefish chocolates are paired with a black mayonnaise made with cuttlefish ink, so as to reprise the theme of cuttlefish and, so to speak, close the circle, in tune with the concept of the dish itself.

Sweets to the Sweet: The Dessert

The common saying was that a good pastry chef can become a good chef, but not vice versa. Even important restaurants had a similar problem, that is the dessert did not reflect the same idea of the kitchen, and was not up to the rest of the meal. It's a different school of thought: pastry is based on extreme precision in the dosage of ingredients, and the creative side, which is much more evident in a chef, is necessarily subject to strict rules. Consequently, many fine dining restaurants used to have a distinct pastry chef who takes care of the sweet part of the menu, and some still do.

Whereas Francesco had to start from scratch with desserts too, in order to learn the basics.

The whole method is different, and I had to read and learn a lot, to document myself on sweets, ice-creams, sorbets. Again, it was a trial-and-error process. I did not know what a *pate à bombe* was, I did not know how to make a parfait, or what caramel was, and why once it was made it turned soft again. Only with time I discovered how humidity and excess moisture affect it, and I found out about the different temperatures when making chocolate according to the different percentage of cocoa, the crystallization of sugars, and so on...

Even though each of its ten provinces has many dessert specialties, the typical Tuscan sweets are dry ones. Some are akin to waffles and biscuits: namely, *"ricciarelli"* (which originated in Siena), the *"brigidini di Lamporecchio"* (near Pistoia), thin and crispy waffles, rounded and curled, gold-orange in color, with a diameter of about 3 inches, made with eggs, sugar, anise or fennel seeds, and very little water and flour; or the *cantucci*, crunchy and filled with almonds, hazelnuts and pine nuts, which must be dipped in Vin santo, a dessert wine made with dried grapes. Or else there are cakes or pies, such as the *Buccellato* of Lucca (a cake made of a sweet and soft pastry, with raisins and aniseed), Pisa's *"Torta co' 'bischeri'"* (a pie

Appendix

filled with rice cocoa, eggs, sugar, pine nuts, candies, raisins and spices), Siena's *"Panforte"* (a traditional Christmas cake, rich in candied fruit and spices and flavored with cloves, cinnamon, pepper, nutmeg and coriander). Traditional desserts often belong to a particular period of the year, or a festivity, such as the *Panettone* in Milan, or the *Pandoro* in Verona, during the Christmas holidays. For instance, Livorno's Easter *"schiacciata,"* which is very similar to Panettone, Florence's *"Schiacciata alla Fiorentina,"* a spongy cake consumed during the Carnival, or Arezzo's *"Panina,"* an Easter cake which can be found in a sweet and a salty version; the latter, called *'unta'* (greasy), is enriched with bacon, which must be eaten with hard-boiled eggs—blessed by the priest during the Easter mass—and salami.

Perhaps the most elaborate dessert is Florence's *Zuccotto*, born during the Renaissance period, and one of the very few moist cakes in the Tuscan tradition: the then-Queen of France, Caterina de' Medici, gave a rich banquet in Florence to welcome the Spanish ambassadors, and asked the famous pastry chef Bernardo Buontalenti to invent a new recipe. Buontalenti, one of the most noted intellectuals of the second half of the 16th century, was also the inventor of ice cream. He came up with a parfait initially called *Elmo di Caterina* (Caterina's Elm), because it was believed to have been made using an infantry elm as mold; the name was later changed into *zuccotto*. The initial version was quite different from the one that can be found nowadays: the base consisted of ricotta cheese, cocoa nib, candied citrus fruits, and an outside layer of sponge cake soaked in Alchermes (a typical Tuscan liquor made by infusing neutral spirits with sugar, cinnamon, cloves, nutmeg and vanilla, with a striking scarlet color obtained by the addition of a coloring agent derived from the Kermes, a small parasitic insect), very much loved by the Medici family.

As Bracali points out, the regional desserts often originated from the necessity to make the best out of poor ingredients as well as from the limits of homemade cooking.

Remember that even the *zuppa inglese* or the *tiramisù* were born as a way to reuse the remains of dry sweets from the previous festivities. Hence the habit of dipping ladyfingers in Alchermes or coffee, in order to soften them. What is more, home kitchens did not have the ovens able to bake cakes at such high temperatures. During the Christmas and Easter festivities, my grandma used to prepare the *pinolata*, a soft cake similar to a donut cake and covered with pine nuts, and one which she called *pesce* (fish), but was actually a *"gattò"* (from the French gateaux), that is a cake sprinkled with Alchermes, cream and chocolate and rolled up. And we used to bring her cakes to the bakery, and the baker would put them into his own oven, because we just could not cook them at home. Most housewives in Massa Marittima used to bring their cakes there, and for us kids it was an event. I remember this big, paunchy dude in a white t-shirt, covered with flour and sweat, offering us a slice of cake, or freshly baked meringues (which we called *spumine*).

For a fine dining restaurant in Tuscany, then, to draw from the regional tradition as regards with desserts is not simple: Either you make your own revisiting of a typical dessert recipe (such as Gaetano Trovato does with his version of the *zuccotto*) and add it your own personality to it, or you can feel free to follow your own whims, based on ingredients:

> For instance, desserts based on, say, strawberries, do not belong to any region, and normally desserts are based on a key ingredient, whether it be chocolate, dry cakes, parfaits. My very first attempts consisted in reinterpretation of such dishes; for instance, I did a molten chocolate cake that was basically a reinterpretation of Michel Bras' *biscuit coulant*, which nowadays you can even find in supermarkets but back then was something quite original. I learnt how to make it by Maurizio Santin, the son of Ezio Santin, who had this dish in the menu at his historical *Antica Osteria del Ponte*, a three-Michelin-stars restaurant from 1986 to 1993, and added some personal elements to it. Then, with time, as I acquired more self-assurance, I felt I could let my own imagination loose.

As a result, his desserts are also original and intriguing. The "corn and yogurt ice cream boat" is "a pulp dessert, unexpectedly self-ironic, like in cleverly orchestrated showdowns" (Fiordelli), while *"L'Autunno"* (Autumn) is a virtuoso exhibition of different textures around the concept enunciated by the title: a fruits and vegetables soup, glazed chestnuts, a vinegar jelly (essential to the balance of the dish), a mango and ginger sorbet, a "ground" of pistachios and cocoa and powdered orange. Other desserts are variations around a basic ingredient, such as chocolate, berries or yogurt, which is presented in different textures or preparations.

A creation Francesco is especially proud of is a dessert presented at the Festa a Vico in 2015, *"Lo yogurt incontra il mare"* (Yogurt Meets the Sea). "Nowadays, the tendency in cooking has been toward acidity and bitterness—a tendency I personally do not embrace—whereas in pastry there has been a decrease in the use of sugar and the advent of savory elements, which is quite interesting. Hence, the basic idea behind this dessert."

The dish is centered around several preparations featuring yogurt. "It is a mixture of classical pastry, technique, and also creativity, the latter allowed by the addition of the savory part of the dessert." Classical pastry is given by the basis, which is a silky, pudding-like yogurt cremoso, made

Appendix

One of Bracali's desserts, "*Lo yogurt incontra il mare*" (Yogurt Meets the Sea).

with white chocolate, egg whites, lyophilized and fresh yogurt. At the center we have and rosemary flavored yogurt ice-cream "It is never easy to make an ice cream with cheese or similar, because they have a fat part and a watery part. To make the ice cream, I leave the yogurt to drain for 24 hours in a sieve, covered with etamine gauze, so that the yogurt loses completely its liquid. Then I replace it partly with a syrup made with water, fructose and rosemary infusion." The technique is represented by a yogurt sponge. It is made with almond flour, lyophilized yogurt and egg white, siphoned in a plastic glass which is then put for just 30 seconds in the microwave oven. It swells and acquires a light, slightly acidic-tasting sponge. Then there is a black yogurt crumble, colored with vegetable carbon, which adds the friable part to the dish. The creative part of the dish, the savory one, is given by the use of seaweed.

> I took seaweeds, washed them but not thoroughly, because I wanted the salty part to be rather present, and vacuum cooked them in a water-and-sugar syrup in the steam oven for 10 minutes. Then I drain them, and put them in a dryer. The seaweed must be turned upside down often, in order for it not to stick to the dryer when the sugar coating crystallizes. The seaweeds add a salty taste which is imme-

diately felt by our taste buds. It reactivates them, even after a particularly opulent meal, and gives the dessert a lighter feeling.

It is a proper conclusion to the menu, and yet another confirmation of the chef's style and vision. Overall, Enzo Vizzari's words, in a 2014 article on *L'Espresso*, are perhaps the most apt synthesis of what is, today, Francesco Bracali's art.

Simple things, or those that seem simple—of course, he can do them. But it is evident that those stimulate him less than the complex dishes, built on playing with many ingredients, to the limits of baroque, and sometimes beyond. Francesco is the personification of the axiom that in the kitchen only a few "prodigies" can afford to be creative, and therefore the vast majority of chefs would better apply to "normality." Such an axiom leads to another: creativity, the real one, is synonymous with maturity.

Index

Index

Index